# Paris



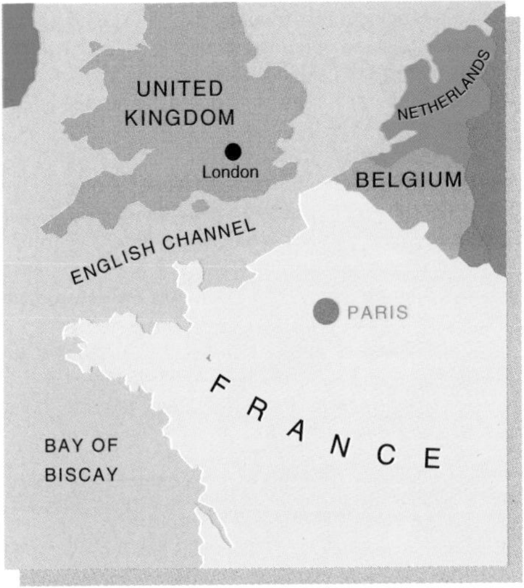


DIAMOND BOOKS

**The blue section** answers the question 'I would like to see or do something; where do I go and what do I see when I get there?' This section is arranged as an alphabetical list of topics. Within each topic you will find:

- A selection of the best examples on offer.
- How to get there, costs and opening hours for each entry.
- The outstanding features of each entry.
- A simplified map, with each entry plotted and the nearest landmark or transport access.

**The red section** is a lively and informative gazetteer. It offers:

- Essential facts about the main places and cultural items. What is La Bastille? Who was Michelangelo? Where is Delphi?

**The gold section** is full of practical and invaluable travel information. It offers:

- Everything you need to know to help you enjoy yourself and get the most out of your time away, from Accommodation through Baby-sitters, Car Hire, Food, Health, Money, Newspapers, Taxis, Telephones to Youth Hostels.

**Cross-references:**

Type in small capitals – CHURCHES – tells you that more information on an item is available within the topic on churches.

**A-Z** after an item tells you that more information is available within the gazetteer. Simply look under the appropriate name.

A name in bold – **Holy Cathedral** – also tells you that more information on an item is available in the gazetteer – again simply look up the name.

# CONTENTS

## PRACTICAL INFORMATION GAZETTEER

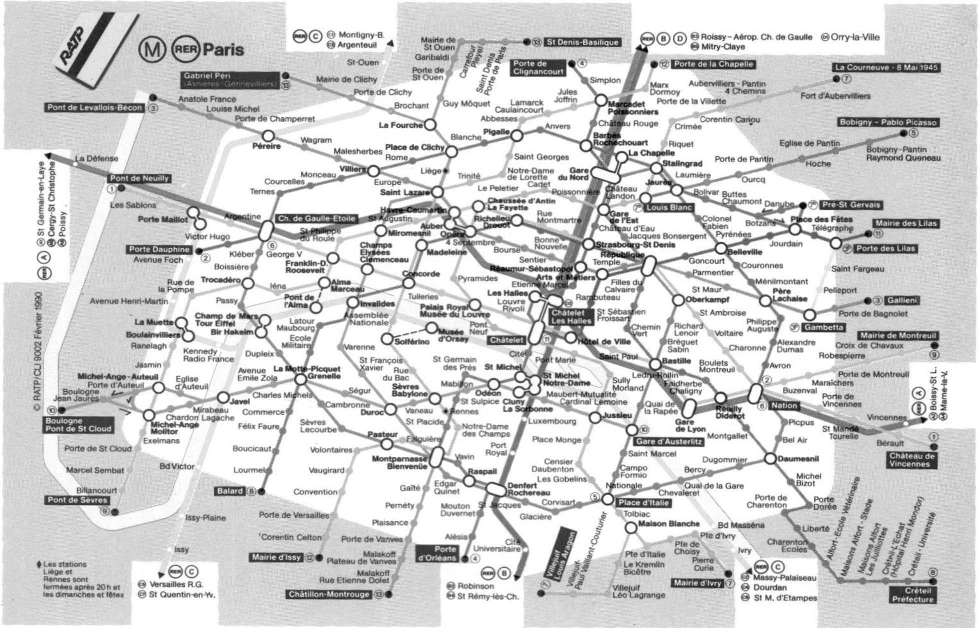

RATP
M RER Paris
RER C Montigny-B. Argenteuil
RER B D Roissy – Aérop. Ch. de Gaulle Orry-la-Ville Mitry-Claye
St Denis-Basilique
Porte de Clignancourt
Porte de la Chapelle
La Courneuve - 8 Mai 1945
Bobigny – Pablo Picasso
Gabriel Péri (Asnières-Gennevilliers)
Pont de Levallois-Bécon
Mairie de St Ouen
Garibaldi
Porte de St Ouen
Carrefour Pleyel
Saint Denis Porte de Paris
St-Ouen
Mairie de Clichy
Porte de Clichy
Anatole France
Louise Michel
Porte de Champerret
Brochant
Guy Môquet
Lamarck Caulaincourt
Jules Joffrin
Simplon
Marcadet Poissonniers
Marx Dormoy
Aubervilliers - Pantin 4 Chemins
Fort d'Aubervilliers
Porte de la Villette
Corentin Cariou
Crimée
Riquet
Château Rouge
Abbesses
La Fourche
Pigalle
Anvers
Barbès Rochechouart
Péreire
Wagram
Malesherbes
Place de Clichy
Blanche
Rome
La Chapelle
Stalingrad
Eglise de Pantin
Bobigny-Pantin Raymond Queneau
Hoche
Porte de Pantin
Ourcq
Laumière
La Défense
Pont de Neuilly
Les Sablons
Porte Maillot
Villiers
Monceau
Courcelles
Ternes
Europe
Liège
Saint Lazare
Trinité
Saint Georges
Notre-Dame de Lorette
Le Peletier
Cadet
Gare du Nord
Poissonnière
Château Landon
Jaurès
Bolivar
Buttes Chaumont
Danube
Pré-St Gervais
Louis Blanc
Botzaris
Place des Fêtes
Télégraphe
Mairie des Lilas
Porte des Lilas
Argentine
Ch. de Gaulle-Etoile
Havre-Caumartin
St Augustin
Chaussée d'Antin La Fayette
Richelieu Drouot
Rue Montmartre
Gare de l'Est
Château d'Eau
Jacques Bonsergent
Colonel Fabien
Pyrénées
Jourdain
Victor Hugo
Porte Dauphine
Avenue Foch
Kléber
George V
St Philippe du Roule
Miromesnil
Auber
Opéra
4 Septembre
Bonne Nouvelle
Strasbourg-St Denis
Belleville
Boissière
Franklin-D. Roosevelt
Champs Elysées Clemenceau
Madeleine
Bourse
Sentier
Réaumur-Sébastopol
République
Temple
Goncourt
Couronnes
Saint Fargeau
Rue de la Pompe
Trocadéro
Iéna
Alma Marceau
Concorde
Pyramides
Arts et Métiers
Parmentier
Ménilmontant
Pelleport
Avenue Henri-Martin
Passy
Pont de l'Alma
Invalides
Tuileries
Les Halles
Etienne Marcel
Filles du Calvaire
St Maur
Père Lachaise
Gallieni
Porte de Bagnolet
Gambetta
La Muette
Boulainvilliers
Champ de Mars Tour Eiffel
Bir Hakeim
Latour Maubourg
Assemblée Nationale
Palais Royal Musée du Louvre
Louvre Rivoli
Rambuteau
Châtelet Les Halles
St Sébastien Froissart
Oberkampf
St Ambroise
Philippe Auguste
Mairie de Montreuil
Croix de Chavaux
Robespierre
Ranelagh
Kennedy Radio France
Dupleix
Ecole Militaire
Varenne
Solférino
Musée d'Orsay
Pont Neuf
Châtelet
Hôtel de Ville
Chemin Vert
Richard Lenoir
Bréguet Sabin
Voltaire
Charonne
Alexandre Dumas
Jasmin
Michel-Ange - Auteuil
Porte d'Auteuil
Eglise d'Auteuil
Avenue Emile Zola
La Motte-Picquet Grenelle
St François Xavier
Rue du Bac
St Germain des Prés
St Michel
Cité
Pont Marie
Saint Paul
Bastille
Boulets Montreuil
Avron
Porte de Montreuil
Maraîchers
Boulogne Jean Jaurès
Boulogne Pont de St Cloud
Michel-Ange Molitor
Mirabeau
Chardon Lagache
Javel
Charles Michels
Ségur
Sèvres Babylone
Mabillon
Odéon
St Michel Notre-Dame
Sully Morland
Ledru-Rollin
Faidherbe Chaligny
Reuilly Diderot
Nation
Buzenval
Porte de Vincennes
Vincennes
RER A Boissy-St L. Marne-la-V.
Exelmans
Commerce
Cambronne
Duroc
Vaneau
St Sulpice
Rennes
Cluny La Sorbonne
Maubert-Mutualité
Cardinal Lemoine
Jussieu
Quai de la Rapée
Gare de Lyon
Picpus
St Mandé Tourelle
Bérault
Château de Vincennes
Porte de St Cloud
Félix Faure
Sèvres Lecourbe
St Placide
Notre-Dame des Champs
Luxembourg
Gare d'Austerlitz
Montgallet
Bel Air
Marcel Sembat
Bd Victor
Boucicaut
Pasteur
Volontaires
Falguière
Montparnasse Bienvenüe
Vavin
Port Royal
Place Monge
Saint Marcel
Dugommier
Daumesnil
Michel Bizot
Lourmel
Vaugirard
Raspail
Edgar Quinet
Censier Daubenton
Les Gobelins
Campo Formio
Bercy
Billancourt
Pont de Sèvres
Balard
Convention
Gaîté
Denfert Rochereau
Nationale
Quai de la Gare
Chevaleret
Porte de Charenton
Porte Dorée
Issy-Plaine
Porte de Versailles
Pernety
Mouton Duvernet
St Jacques
Corvisart
Place d'Italie
Glacière
Tolbiac
Bd Masséna
Liberté
Alfort-Ecole Vétérinaire
Maisons Alfort - Stade
Maisons Alfort Les Juilliottes
Créteil-L'Echat (Hôpital Henri Mondor)
Créteil - Université
Créteil Préfecture
Issy
Corentin Celton
Plaisance
Porte de Vanves
Alésia
Cité Universitaire
Villejuif Louis Aragon
Villejuif-Paul Vaillant-Couturier
Maison Blanche
Pte d'Ivry
Porte d'Italie
Le Kremlin Bicêtre
Pte de Choisy
Pierre Curie
Ivry
Charenton Ecoles
Mairie d'Issy
Malakoff Plateau de Vanves
Malakoff Rue Etienne Dolet
Châtillon-Montrouge
Porte d'Orléans
RER B Robinson St Rémy-lès-Ch.
Villejuif Léo Lagrange
Mairie d'Ivry
RER C Massy-Palaiseau Dourdan St M. d'Etampes
RER C Versailles R.G. St Quentin-en-Yv.
RER A St Germain-en-Laye Cergy-St Christophe Poissy
♦ Les stations Liège et Rennes sont fermées après 20 h et les dimanches et fêtes
© RATP/CLI 9002 Février 1990

# INTRODUCTION

Paris brings the senses to life. As you walk through its streets and along its boulevards luscious displays of fish and oysters outside the brasseries tempt you. You will also be tempted by the pastries displayed in the patisseries, and as you pass the pavement cafés the smell of coffee and brioches, and the cheerful clatter of that thick china on their zinc tabletops, lures you in so that before long, you'll be forced to sit down at one of those tables. And, sitting at a table in one of the city's famous cafés with your coffee or *citron*, you can indulge in the famous Parisian pastime of watching people going about their business.

And sooner or later, as you make your way about the city on the clean and efficient Métro, or as you stroll along the boulevards created by Napoleon's Baron Haussmann, past shop windows in which elegance is sold as nowhere else, and among the people of whom that elegance is a hallmark, you can't help noticing the style and self-possession of the locals. Style is the birthright of the *parisian* and *parisienne*.

Paris is aptly named the 'City of Light', and to confirm that you will do well to go to the Musée d'Orsay where Impressionist and other French painters of the late 19thC and early 20thC are now displayed in what was once the Gare d'Orsay, an old railway station. Among the superb displays of sculpture and paintings (and for the Impressionists the interpretation of light was of paramount importance) you will see more style and begin to realize how Paris has passed on this inheritance to its present-day citizens.

Paris is full of galleries and museums – the Musée du Louvre is within 500 m of the Pont Royal across the Seine, but you might not want to go there so soon after the Musée d'Orsay! Instead stay on the Left Bank, walk upstream and turn right at pl. St. Michel onto bd. St. Michel. Here you will find yourself in the heart of the Latin Quarter, the setting for Puccini's *La Bohème*. Here too you can see the history of Paris, in the form of medieval houses, and the beautiful church of St. Séverin, begun in the 13thC, enlarged in the 16thC and then decorated in the 17th and 18thC. And of course this area is home to the Sorbonne, one of the oldest, and still one of the leading, universities in the world.

Across bd. St. Germain is the Musée de Cluny, a 15thC house of great beauty which now holds a collection of incomparable tapestries,

among them a group of six called *Lady with the Unicorn*, which represent the five senses. By this time you will have gained a feel for the city and in the days to come you will hopefully be ready to relax and soak up the atmosphere.

What could be more atmospheric than the open-air markets: the flea market out at Clignancourt, held at the weekend, which sells everything from clothes to antiques; and, in the true centre of Paris, where the city began, the beautiful flower market on the Île de la Cité. But the *grands magasins* will give you a different impression of French commerce. Even if you don't buy anything, the architecture alone in Galeries Lafayette is worth a visit.

A walk along the Seine and on the Île de la Cité brings you to the cathedral of Notre-Dame de Paris, one of the finest flowerings of French Gothic architecture. Along with the Arc de Triomphe and the Eiffel Tower, Notre Dame is one of the symbols of Paris. A cliché perhaps but France coined the word cliché, and what's in a name? There are certain clichés about a visit to Paris which are more than worth your while: Montmartre, home of the Moulin Rouge whose performers and habitués became the subjects of Toulouse-Lautrec's sketches and where you can still see the cancan performed, where the gleaming Sacré-Coeur church dominates the height, and where artists set up their easels on the street; the Eiffel Tower, from whose three stages there are positively giddy views; the nearby Trocadéro with its gardens, where

you might eat your lunch of French bread, pâté and cheese, and watch the fountains glitter in the sun; and how about a cruise along the river on a *bateau-mouche*. And last but not least, a visit to Versailles, the glorious palace of the Sun King, Louis XIV.

But it would be a mistake to make a visit to Paris one long sightseeing trip. Better to take in some of the treasures of the city and then make it your own, to go out to Neuilly for no particular reason except to be in a Paris suburb, to go to the Bois de Boulogne simply to wander among the trees, to spend the morning sitting in cafés, go to one of innumerable restaurants for lunch, go to the cinema, the theatre, a disco or nightclub.

Remember these things: if you like your steak medium ask for it *bien cuit*, because in France they like their meat rarer, on the whole, than the British do; and that if you go to one of the big-reputation bars the drinks may cost you more than you want to pay!

Lastly, prepare to be offended now and then by the ungiving eye of the Parisian in the street, and not to take it personally, because offence is seldom being given. It is just that to the inhabitants of the city Paris is the only place to be and they know it too. If you doubted it you would simply be asked, where else is there? So just relax and soak up the atmosphere of romance, history, style and glamour which is Paris, City of Light.

***William Watson***

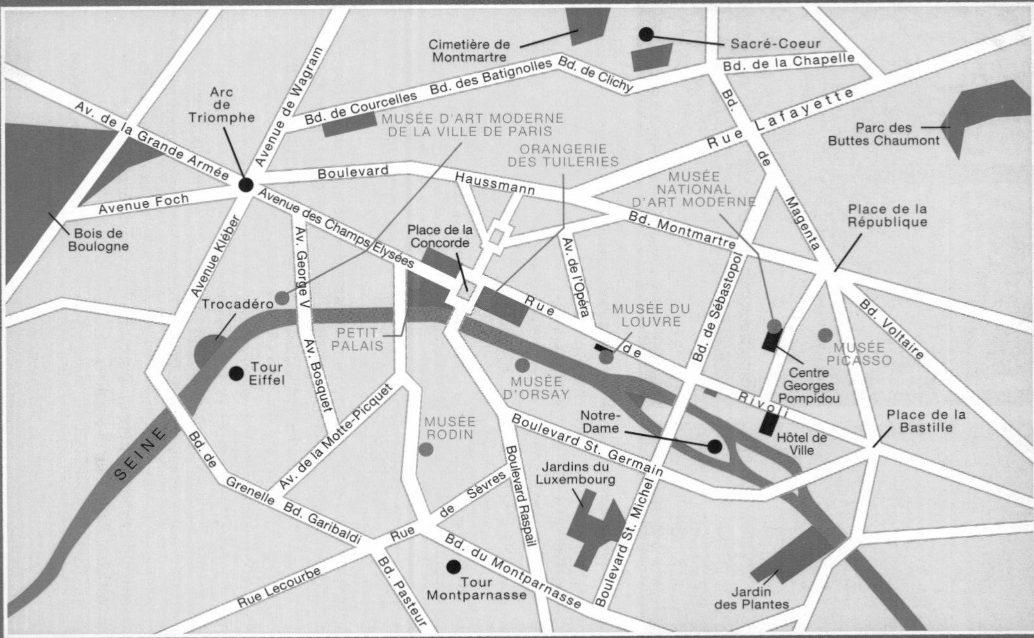

Cimetière de Montmartre
Sacré-Coeur
Bd. de la Chapelle
Bd. de Courcelles
Bd. des Batignolles
Bd. de Clichy
Arc de Triomphe
Avenue de Wagram
Av. de la Grande Armée
MUSÉE D'ART MODERNE DE LA VILLE DE PARIS
Parc des Buttes Chaumont
Rue Lafayette
Boulevard Haussmann
ORANGERIE DES TUILERIES
MUSÉE NATIONAL D'ART MODERNE
Avenue Foch
Avenue des Champs Elysées
Bd. de Magenta
Bois de Boulogne
Place de la Concorde
Bd. Montmartre
Place de la République
Avenue Kléber
Av. George V
Av. de l'Opéra
Bd. de Sébastopol
Trocadéro
Rue de Rivoli
MUSÉE DU LOUVRE
Bd. Voltaire
PETIT PALAIS
MUSÉE PICASSO
Tour Eiffel
Av. Bosquet
MUSÉE D'ORSAY
Centre Georges Pompidou
Av. de la Motte-Picquet
Notre-Dame
Place de la Bastille
MUSÉE RODIN
Boulevard St. Germain
Hôtel de Ville
SEINE
Bd. de Grenelle
Jardins du Luxembourg
Rue de Sèvres
Boulevard Raspail
Bd. Garibaldi
Boulevard St. Michel
Bd. du Montparnasse
Bd. Pasteur
Tour Montparnasse
Rue Lecourbe
Jardin des Plantes

**MUSÉE DU LOUVRE** Palais du Louvre, 1er.
■ 0900-1800 Thu.-Sun., 0900-2145 Mon. & Wed. M Louvre, Palais Royal. ● 30F (15F Sun.).
*Probably one of the world's foremost art collections. See* **MUSTS**, **A-Z**.

**MUSÉE NATIONAL D'ART MODERNE** Centre Georges Pompidou, rue Beaubourg, 4e. ■ 1200-2200 Sat. & Sun., 1000-2200 Mon. & Wed.-Fri. M Rambuteau, Hôtel de Ville. ● 23F.
*Impressive collection of paintings and sculpture from 1905 onwards.*

**MUSÉE D'ORSAY** 1 rue de Bellechasse, 7e.
■ 1000-1800 Tue.-Sun. (till 2115 Thu.). M/RER Musée d'Orsay.
● 30F (15F Sun.).
*Old Orsay station, now an art gallery for the period 1848-1914. See* **A-Z**.

**ORANGERIE DES TUILERIES** Pl. de la Concorde, 1e.
■ 0945-1715 Wed.-Mon. M Concorde. ● 25F.
*Impressionist and Postimpressionist works.*

**MUSÉE D'ART MODERNE DE LA VILLE DE PARIS**
11 av. du Président Wilson, 16e. ■ 1000-1730 Tue.-Sun. (till 2030 Wed.). M Iéna. ● 15F.
*20thC art; has fine examples of the Cubist and Fauvist movements.*

**PETIT PALAIS** 1 av. Winston Churchill, 8e. ■ 1000-1740 Tue.-Sun.
M Champs Elysées-Clemenceau. ● 12F (special exhibitions 25F).
*Eclectic collection of tapestries, porcelain, Egyptian art, 19thC paintings.*

**MUSÉE PICASSO** 5 rue de Thorigny, 3e. ■ 0915-1715 Wed.-Mon. (till 2200 Wed.). M Chemin Vert, St. Paul. ● 21F.
*Superb range of Picassos, demonstrating his versatility and prolific output, housed in a magnificent 17thC mansion.*

**MUSÉE RODIN** 77 rue de Varenne, 7e.
■ 1000-1700 Tue.-Sun. M Varenne. ● 20F.
*Display of Rodin's works in mansion where he once lived and worked.*

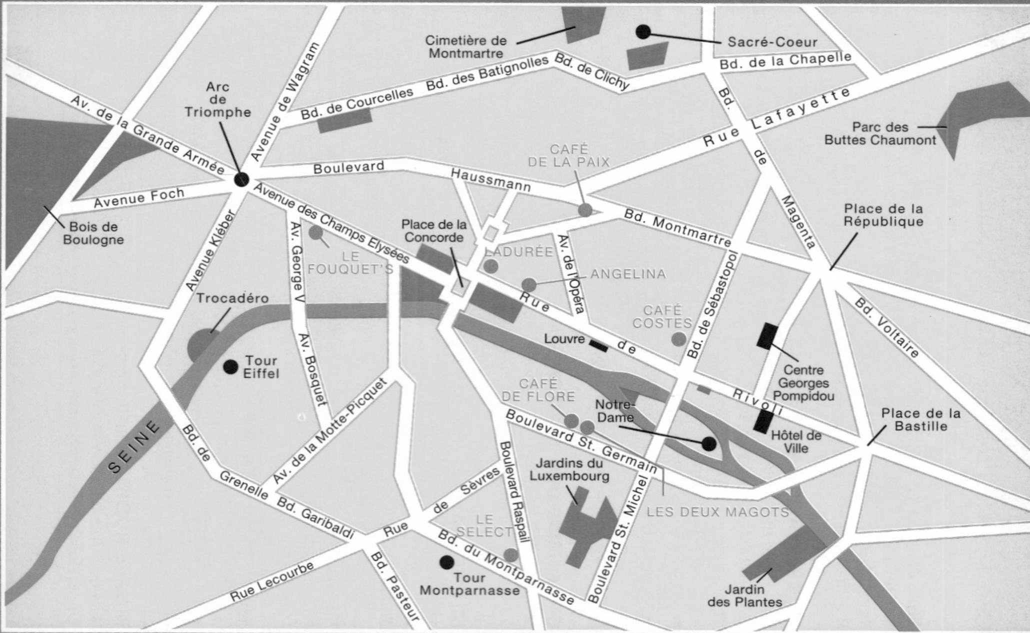
Cimetière de Montmartre
Sacré-Coeur
Bd. de la Chapelle
Bd. de Courcelles
Bd. des Batignolles
Bd. de Clichy
Arc de Triomphe
Avenue de Wagram
Av. de la Grande Armée
Bd.
Rue Lafayette
Parc des Buttes Chaumont
CAFÉ DE LA PAIX
Boulevard
Haussmann
Avenue Foch
Bois de Boulogne
Avenue des Champs Elysées
Place de la Concorde
LADURÉE
Av. de l'Opéra
ANGELINA
Bd. Montmartre
de
Magenta
Place de la République
Avenue Kléber
Av. George V
LE FOUQUET'S
Trocadéro
Tour Eiffel
Rue
Louvre
de
CAFÉ COSTES
Bd. de Sébastopol
Bd. Voltaire
Centre Georges Pompidou
Rivoli
Av. Bosquet
CAFÉ DE FLORE
Notre-Dame
Hôtel de Ville
Place de la Bastille
SEINE
Av. de la Motte-Picquet
Boulevard St. Germain
Bd. de Grenelle
Bd. Garibaldi
Rue de Sèvres
Boulevard Raspail
Jardins du Luxembourg
Boulevard St. Michel
LES DEUX MAGOTS
LE SELECT
Bd. du Montparnasse
Tour Montparnasse
Rue Lecourbe
Bd. Pasteur
Jardin des Plantes

**LE FOUQUET'S** 99 av. des Champs Elysées, 8e.
■ 1030-2400 Mon.-Fri. M George V. ● Coffee 25F, à la carte 400F.
*A Parisian institution – the French César film awards are celebrated here each year. See* **WALK 4**.

**CAFÉ DE LA PAIX** 12 bd. des Capucines, 9e.
■ 1200-0115. M Opéra. ● Coffee 17F, à la carte 180F.
*Typical pavement café, with superb Napoleon III décor.*

**LES DEUX MAGOTS** 6 pl. St. Germain-des-Prés, 6e.
■ 0730-0100. M St. Germain-des-Prés. ● Coffee 19F.
The *place for an elegant breakfast. See* **WALK 3**.

**CAFÉ DE FLORE** 172 bd. St. Germain, 6e.
■ 0700-0130. M St. Germain-des-Prés. ● Coffee 19F.
*This café is famous as the favourite haunt of 30s literary figures.*

**LE SELECT** 99 bd. du Montparnasse, 6e.
■ 0830-0230. M Vavin. ● Coffee 12F.
*The last American bar in Montparnasse (see* **A-Z***) where intellectuals and artists still congregate.*

**CAFÉ COSTES** Pl. des Innocents, 1er.
■ 0830-0200. M Les Halles, RER Châtelet-Les Halles. ● Coffee 14F.
*Ultra-chic café-bar with an interior designed by Philippe Starck. Check out the toilets!*

**LADURÉE** 16 rue Royale, 8e.
■ 0830-1900 Mon.-Sat. Lunch 1130-1500. M Madeleine.
● Tea 23F, Coffee 14F, Cakes 17-23F, Lunch 60-80F (plat du jour).
*Spoil yourself with the delicious variety of cakes and wide range of teas.*

**ANGELINA** 226 rue de Rivoli, 1er.
■ 0900-1900. M Tuileries. ● Coffee 15F.
*One of the most chic* salons de thé *in Paris. Its speciality is the Mont Blanc, meringue covered in whipped chestnut cream.*

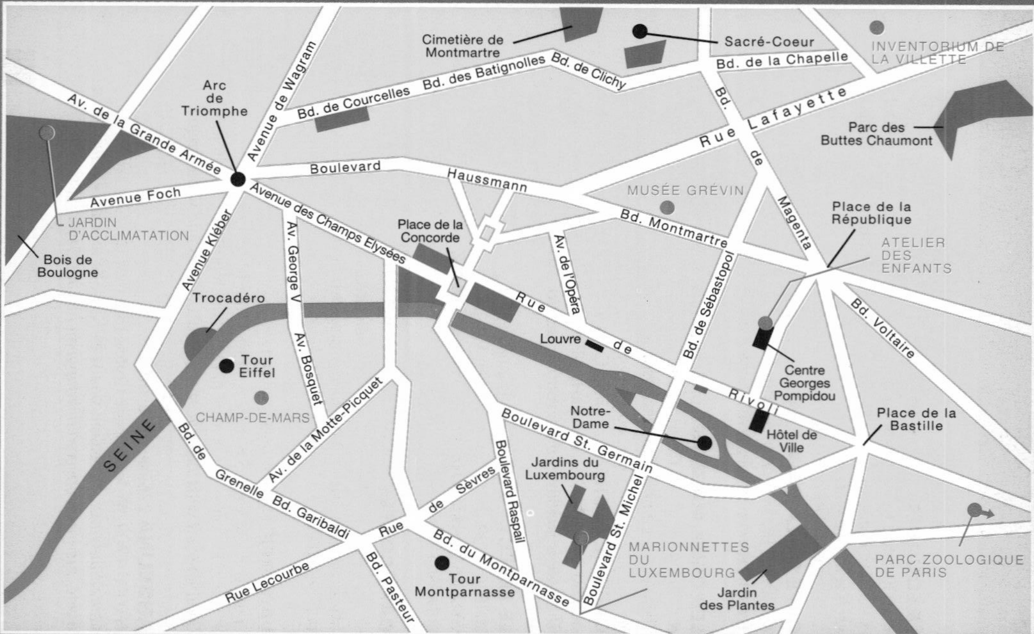
Cimetière de Montmartre
Sacré-Coeur
Inventorium de la Villette
Bd. de la Chapelle
Bd. de Courcelles
Bd. des Batignolles
Bd. de Clichy
Arc de Triomphe
Avenue de Wagram
Av. de la Grande Armée
Rue Lafayette
Parc des Buttes Chaumont
Boulevard Haussmann
Avenue Foch
Musée Grévin
Bd. de Magenta
Jardin d'Acclimatation
Bois de Boulogne
Avenue Kléber
Avenue des Champs Elysées
Av. George V
Place de la Concorde
Av. de l'Opéra
Bd. Montmartre
Place de la République
Atelier des Enfants
Trocadéro
Rue de Rivoli
Louvre
Bd. de Sébastopol
Bd. Voltaire
Tour Eiffel
Av. Bosquet
Centre Georges Pompidou
Champ-de-Mars
Notre-Dame
Place de la Bastille
Hôtel de Ville
Seine
Av. de la Motte-Picquet
Boulevard St. Germain
Bd. de Grenelle
Boulevard Raspail
Jardins du Luxembourg
Rue de Sèvres
Bd. Garibaldi
Boulevard St. Michel
Marionnettes du Luxembourg
Jardin des Plantes
Parc Zoologique de Paris
Rue Lecourbe
Bd. Pasteur
Tour Montparnasse
Bd. du Montparnasse

**PARC ZOOLOGIQUE DE PARIS** 53 av. de St. Maurice, 12e.
■ 0900-1730. M Porte Dorée. ● 35F.
*Over 200 species – don't miss the lemur house. See* **Bois de Vincennes**.

**ATELIER DES ENFANTS** Centre Georges Pompidou, Beaubourg, 4e. ■ 1200-2200 Sat. & Sun., 1000-2200 Mon. & Wed.-Fri.
M Rambuteau, Hôtel de Ville. ● Free.
*Creative workshops for children aged five and over.*

**JARDIN D'ACCLIMATATION** Bois de Boulogne, 16e.
■ 1000-1800. M Sablons. ● 7,50F.
*Enormous park providing playgrounds, a miniature railway, go-karts, an 'enchanted river' and a zoo. See* **Bois de Boulogne**.

**MARIONNETTES DU LUXEMBOURG** Jardins du Luxembourg, 6e. ■ 1430 & 1530 Wed.-Sat., 1430, 1530 & 1630 Sun. M Vavin.
● 20F.
*Very popular puppet show with an extensive repertoire.*

**CHAMP-DE-MARS** 7e.
■ 24 hr. M Ecole Militaire. ● Free.
*The park next to the Tour Eiffel (see* **A-Z***), with pony rides, a puppet theatre and picnic areas.*

**MUSÉE GRÉVIN** 10 bd. Montmartre, 9e.
■ 1300-1900 (from 1000 during school hols). M Rue Montmartre.
● 46F, child 32F.
*Waxworks museum founded in 1882, which contains displays depicting episodes from French history.*

**INVENTORIUM DE LA VILLETTE** Cité des Sciences et de l'Industrie, 30 av. Corentin Cariou, 19e. ■ Film at 1100, 1230, 1400 & 1530. M Corentin Cariou. ● 15F.
*The Géode, in the city, houses the only cinema in France with a hemispherical screen measuring 1000 sq. m. There are 1.5 hr film and water-game workshops for children aged 3-12. See* **MUSEUMS 3**.

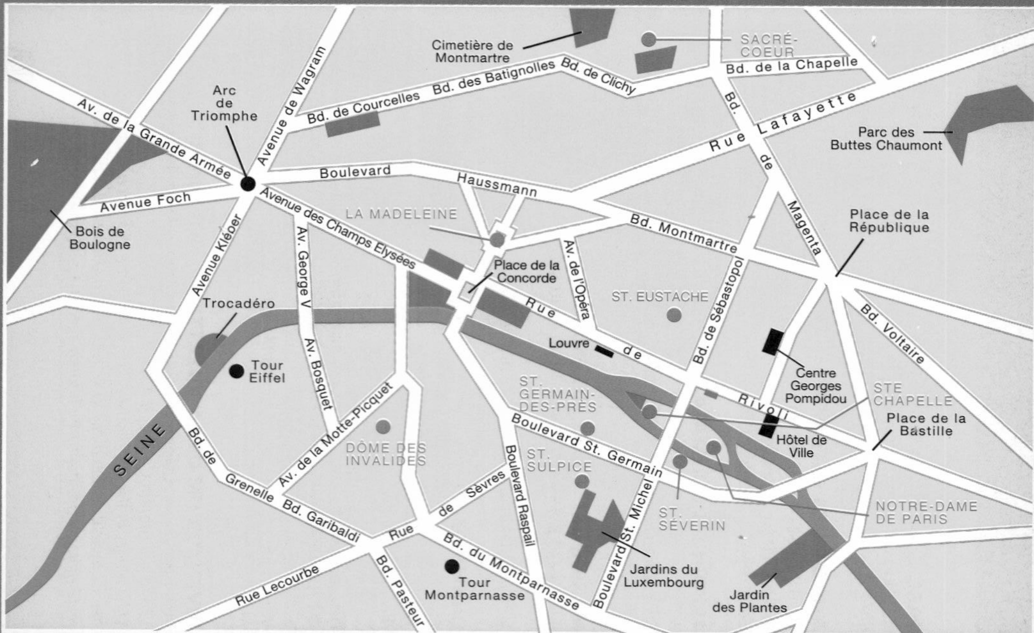

Parc des Buttes Chaumont
Place de la République
Bd. Voltaire
Place de la Bastille
STE CHAPELLE
NOTRE-DAME DE PARIS
SACRÉ-COEUR
Bd. de la Chapelle
Rue Lafayette
Bd. de Magenta
Centre Georges Pompidou
Hôtel de Ville
Rivoli
Jardin des Plantes
Bd. de Sébastopol
Bd. Montmartre
ST. EUSTACHE
ST. SEVERIN
Cimetière de Montmartre
Bd. de Clichy
Bd. des Batignolles
Rue de Louvre
Boulevard St. Michel
Jardins du Luxembourg
Av. de l'Opéra
ST. GERMAIN-DES-PRES
Boulevard St. Germain
ST. SULPICE
Place de la Concorde
Boulevard Haussmann
Boulevard Raspail
Bd. du Montparnasse
Rue de Sevres
Tour Montparnasse
LA MADELEINE
Bd. de Courcelles
Avenue des Champs Elysées
DÔME DES INVALIDES
Av. de la Motte-Picquet
Bd. Pasteur
Av. George V
Av. Bosquet
Bd. Garibaldi
Avenue de Wagram
Arc de Triomphe
Tour Eiffel
Trocadéro
Avenue Kléber
Bd. de Grenelle
Rue Lecourbe
Av. de la Grande Armée
Avenue Foch
SEINE
Bois de Boulogne

**NOTRE-DAME DE PARIS** Pl. du Parvis Notre-Dame, 4e.
■ 0800-1900. M Cité. ● Free.
*Famous masterpiece of French Gothic architecture. See* **A-Z**.

**SACRÉ-COEUR** 36 rue du Chevalier-de-la-Barre, 18e.
■ 0630-2300. M Anvers, Abbesses. ● Free.
*The prominent white domes are one of the city's most familiar landmarks. See* **A-Z**.

**STE CHAPELLE** Bd. du Palais, 1er.
■ 1000-1620. M Cité. ● 23F, inc. entry to La Conciergerie (see **A-Z**).
*Best known for its superb stained-glass windows. See* **A-Z.**

**LA MADELEINE** Pl. de la Madeleine, 8e.
■ 0800-1800. M Madeleine. ● Free.
*Built for Napoleon (see* **A-Z***) in the style of a Greek temple. See* **WALK 4**.

**ST. SULPICE** Pl. St. Sulpice, 6e.
■ 0730-1700. M St. Sulpice, Mabillon. ● Free.
*Famous for its music: regular recitals on Europe's largest organ. See* **A-Z**.

**ST. SÉVERIN** 1 rue des Prêtres St. Séverin, 5e.
■ 1100-1930 Mon.-Sat., 0900-2000 Sun. M/RER St. Michel. ● Free.
*University church, late Gothic with modern stained glass.*

**ST. GERMAIN-DES-PRÉS** Pl. St. Germain-des-Prés, 6e.
■ 0745-1930. M St. Germain-des-Prés. ● Free.
*Oldest church in Paris (11th-12thC); hosts splendid concerts. See* **A-Z**.

**DÔME DES INVALIDES** Av. de Tourville, 7e.
■ 0900-1800. M Ecole Militaire, Varenne, Invalides. ● Free.
*Impressive church with magnificent dome; Napoleon's tomb. See* **A-Z**.

**ST. EUSTACHE** Pl. du Jour, 1er.
■ 0830-1900. M/RER Châtelet-Les Halles. ● Free.
*In Gothic style with Renaissance decoration. Exceptional concerts.*

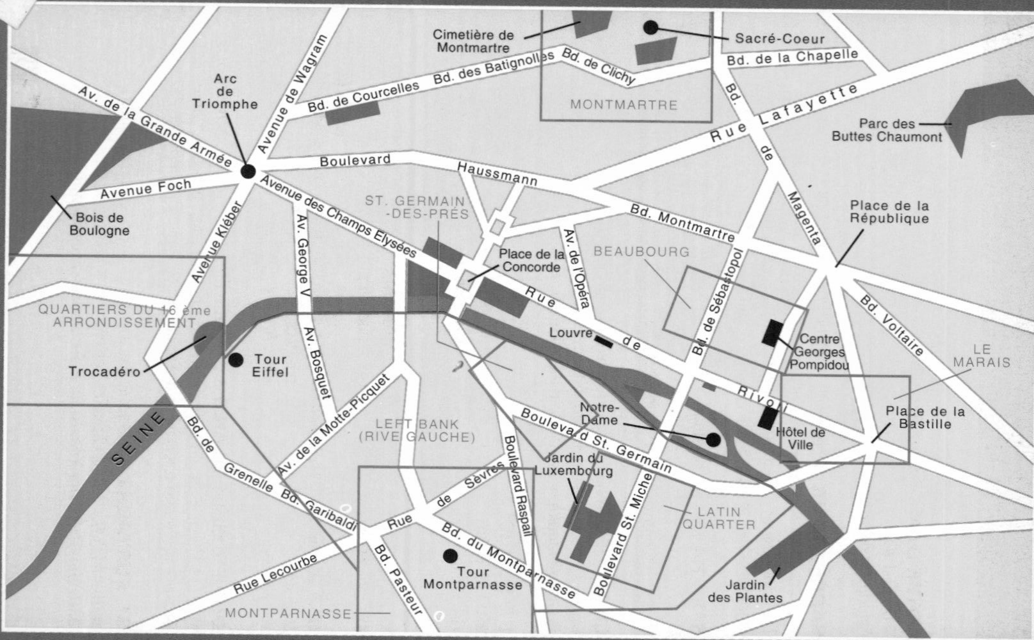
Cimetière de Montmartre
Sacré-Coeur
Bd. de la Chapelle
Arc de Triomphe
Avenue de Wagram
Bd. de Courcelles
Bd. des Batignolles
Bd. de Clichy
MONTMARTRE
Bd.
Rue Lafayette
Parc des Buttes Chaumont
Av. de la Grande Armée
Boulevard Haussmann
de
Avenue Foch
Bois de Boulogne
Avenue Kléber
Av. George V
Avenue des Champs Elysées
ST. GERMAIN -DES-PRÉS
Bd. Montmartre
Magenta
Place de la République
Place de la Concorde
Av. de l'Opéra
BEAUBOURG
Bd. de Sébastopol
Rue de Rivoli
Louvre
QUARTIERS DU 16 ème ARRONDISSEMENT
Trocadéro
Tour Eiffel
Av. Bosquet
Centre Georges Pompidou
Bd. Voltaire
LE MARAIS
Av. de la Motte-Picquet
LEFT BANK (RIVE GAUCHE)
Notre-Dame
Boulevard St. Germain
Place de la Bastille
Hôtel de Ville
SEINE
Bd. de Grenelle
Bd. Garibaldi
Rue de Sèvres
Boulevard Raspail
Jardin du Luxembourg
Boulevard St. Miche
LATIN QUARTER
Rue Lecourbe
Bd. Pasteur
Tour Montparnasse
Bd. du Montparnasse
Jardin des Plantes
MONTPARNASSE

**BEAUBOURG** RER Châtelet-Les Halles.
*1er, between Les Halles and rue Beaubourg. Home of Centre Pompidou (see* **A-Z***) and a popular shopping area, with trendy cafés and bars.*

**QUARTIERS DU 16ème ARRONDISSEMENT**
M Eglise d'Auteuil, Trocadéro.
*16e and southern 17e* arrondissements *(see* **A-Z***). Wealthy area next to Bois de Boulogne (see* **A-Z***). To the north is av. Foch, Paris' equivalent of Sloane Sq.; to the south are the village-like areas of Auteuil and Passy.*

**LE MARAIS** M Hôtel de Ville, St. Paul, Bastille.
*3e and 4e, between Beaubourg and pl. de la Bastille (see* **A-Z***). Once aristocratic, it now has museums, libraries and apartments. See* **WALK 2**.

**LEFT BANK (RIVE GAUCHE)** M Odéon, RER St. Michel.
*5e and 6e. South of the Seine (see* **A-Z***), traditionally the haunt of intellectuals, students and bohemians. See* **A-Z**.

**MONTMARTRE** M Anvers, Abbesses, Lamarck Caulaincourt.
*18e. On a steep hill topped by the Sacré-Coeur (see* **A-Z***). Its narrow streets which once attracted famous artists and writers are now very touristy. See* **A-Z**.

**MONTPARNASSE** M Montparnasse Bienvenüe, Raspail.
*6e, 14e and 15e. Similar creative associations to Montmartre (see* **A-Z***), especially between the wars. Nowadays it is dominated by the Maine-Montparnasse complex and Tour Montparnasse. See* **A-Z**.

**LATIN QUARTER** M Odéon, RER St. Michel.
*5e. The Left Bank's spirit is most prevalent in the narrow streets by bd. St. Michel. Pl. St. Michel is popular with tourists and students, and there are many cheaper hotels and restaurants. See* **A-Z**.

**ST. GERMAIN-DES-PRÉS** M St. Germain-des-Prés, Mabillon.
*North part of 6e, around pl. St. Germain-des-Prés. An attractive and lively area, with bookshops, galleries and antique shops.*

CONSULAT
AMBASSADE
SOUPERS
LE CONSULAT

PETIT VERSAILLES
DU MARAIS
Daufin
SAUVEL
AUVEL
BAR BRASSERIE LE FONTENOY

PRODUITS
DE
LA MER
CUISINES
ET
VINS

**ST. DENIS BASILIQUE** Pl. de l'Hôtel de Ville, St. Denis.
1000-1800. M St. Denis Basilique. Free.
*A landmark in European architecture. See* **A-Z**.

**ENGHIEN-LES-BAINS** 10 km north of Paris.
SNCF: Gare du Nord to Enghien.
*This charming town is the nearest waterside resort to Paris. The picturesque lakeside views, boating, games, festivities and casino make it a firm favourite with Parisians.*

**ABBAYE DE ROYAUMONT** Asnières-sur-Oise, Luzarches. 30 km north of Paris. SNCF: Gare du Nord to Luzarches. Car: A 1 then C 909 at La Croix Verte. 1000-1130, 1400-1745 Mar.-Nov. (closed Tue. in Mar., April, Oct. & Nov.); Sat., Sun. & hols (Dec.-Feb.). 18F, under 16, students and OAPs 12F.
*Cistercian abbey founded 1228 by Louis IX, of majestic dimensions but beautiful simplicity. Don't miss refectory – a masterpiece of Gothic art.*

**CHATEAU & MUSÉE CONDÉ** Chantilly. 40 km north of Paris.
SNCF: Gare du Nord to Chantilly. Car: A 1 and turn off at Survilliers.
1000-1800 Wed.-Mon. 30F, under 12 7F (park only 12F, child 7F).
*The Château de Chantilly stands beside a splendid carp-filled lake and houses the Musée Condé. See* **Chantilly**.

**CATHÉDRALE NOTRE-DAME** Senlis. 50 km north of Paris.
SNCF: Gare du Nord to Chantilly, then bus to Senlis. Car: A 1.
*The cathedral, built 1155-84, is contemporary with St. Denis (see* **A-Z***) and Notre-Dame de Paris (see* **A-Z***). Senlis also has the remains of 3rdC city walls and an arena, as well as lovely medieval buildings and streets.*

**PARC ASTÉRIX** Plailly, Oise-en-Picardie. 38 km north of Paris.
SNCF: Gare du Nord to Survilliers-Fosses. Car: A 1. 1000-1900.
145F, child 100F.
*Adventure park on the theme of the well-known comic-strip character. Five main areas – Asterix's World, Rome, Imaginary World, Lake and the Paris street – feature shows, games, exhibitions, restaurants and shops.*

bijoutier
BOULANGERIE
PATISSERIE
PROCHAINEMENT OUVER
d'un GLAC
BOULANGERIE · PATISSERIE
2175·RE 78

**ST. GERMAIN-EN-LAYE** 17 km west of Paris.
RER Line A1. Car: N 13, 190 and 186. ■ 0900-1715 Wed.-Mon. ● 18F.
*Renaissance castle and museum of national antiquities. See* **A-Z**.

**PARC DE ST. CLOUD** 3.5 km west of Paris.
M Boulogne-Pont de St. Cloud. Car: N 307. ● 0700-2200.
*Park designed by Le Nôtre, with fine views overlooking the Seine (see* **A-Z***).*

**MUSÉE NATIONAL DE LA CÉRAMIQUE** Sèvres. 3.5 km west of Paris. M Pont de Sèvres. Car: N 10. ■ 1000-1715 Wed.-Mon. ● 16F.
*Houses numerous collections of Islamic ceramics, varnished pottery, Delftware, French ware, Italian majolica and, of course, Sèvres china.*

**MEUDON** 5 km southwest of Paris.
SNCF: Montparnasse to Versailles Rive-Gauche. Car: N 10.
Musée d'Art et d'Histoire, 11 rue des Pierres.
■ 1400-1800 Wed.-Sun. ● Free.
Musée National Auguste Rodin, 19 av. Auguste Rodin.
■ 1330-1800 Sat.-Mon. ● 8F, 18-25 and OAPs 4F, under 18 free.
*The first museum has local history with a section on 50s and 60s abstract art; sketches, plaster models and Rodin's tomb are in the second.*

**MUSÉE-PROMENADE DE MARLY-LE-ROI** Marly. 17 km southwest of Paris. SNCF: St. Lazare for St. Nom-la-Bretèche. Car: A 13 towards St. Germain-en-Laye. ■ 1400-1800 Wed.-Sun. ● 15F.
*The museum pays tribute to the artistic and literary life of the 19thC, including the Impressionists, who were particularly fond of the grounds.*

**CHATEAU & PARC ZOOLOGIQUE** Thoiry-en-Yvelines. 40 km west of Paris. SNCF: Montparnasse to Montfort-l'Amaury (Dreux train) or Villiers, or RER line C5 to Versailles Rive-Gauche. Car: A 13.
■ 1000-1800 Mon.-Sat., 1000-1900 Sun. ● 73F adult, 59F child for zoo, gardens and African reserve; 96F (82F) with chateau.
*16thC castle housing gastronomy museum. The grounds have been converted into an animal park boasting 800 beasts, including an African reserve (visit by minibus) and beautifully laid out botanical gardens.*

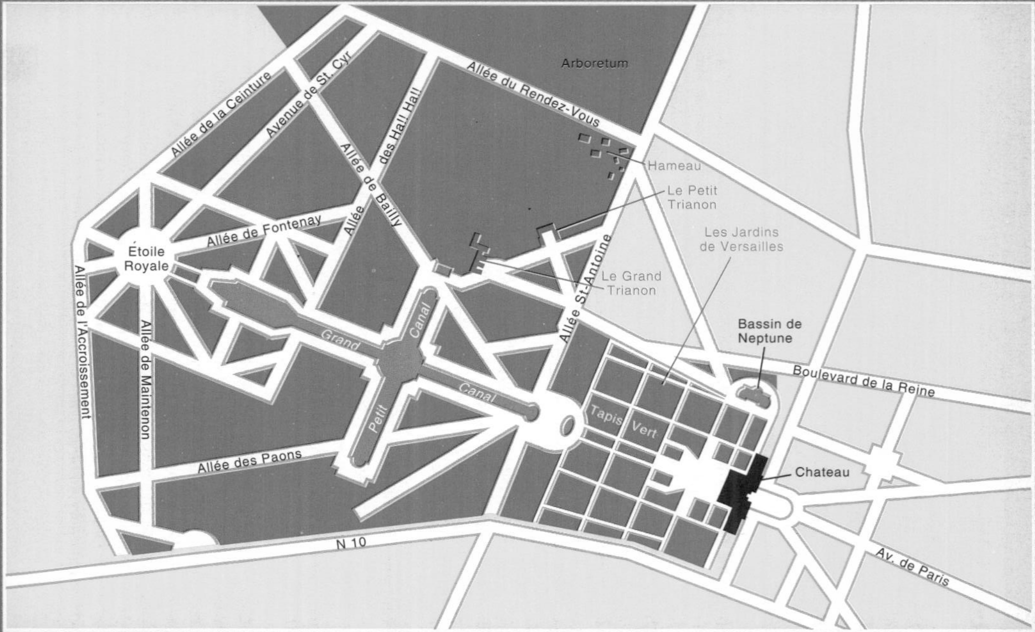
Arboretum
Allée du Rendez-Vous
Allée de la Ceinture
Avenue de St. Cyr
Allée des Ha!! Ha!!
Allée de Bailly
Allée de Fontenay
Hameau
Le Petit Trianon
Le Grand Trianon
Allée St-Antoine
Les Jardins de Versailles
Étoile Royale
Allée de l'Accroissement
Allée de Maintenon
Grand Canal
Petit Canal
Allée des Paons
Tapis Vert
Bassin de Neptune
Boulevard de la Reine
Chateau
N 10
Av. de Paris

## Versailles

*17 km west of Paris.*
*RER line C to Versailles Rive-Gauche, or SNCF from Gare des Invalides, St. Lazare or Montparnasse. M Pont de Sèvres then Bus 171. Car: A 13.*
*Chateau 0900-1700 Tue.-Sun. 30F, reduced rate 15F.*

The main attraction of Versailles (see **A-Z**) is the world-famous 17thC chateau and gardens which housed the French court and government from 1682 until the French Revolution. Originally a small hunting lodge, the building was rebuilt and greatly extended between 1661 and 1720 to become the royal seat of Louis XIV. During the Revolutionary period it was abandoned, then made into a museum in 1837. A visit should include the State Apartments, Hall of Mirrors, Queen's Apartment, Chapel and the historical museum. The King's Suite, Royal Opera and King's Private Apartments can only be visited by guided tour (various tours are available on Tue. and Fri. afternoons at an additional cost of 15F per hr).

**Les Jardins de Versailles.** Laid out by Le Nôtre along two axes, these gardens are a masterpiece of elegance and formality. After visiting the Bassin de Neptune, the most impressive of the gardens, and admiring the view from the central steps, stroll down the Tapis Vert to examine the statues and vases that line the avenue. On your left is the Colonnade (designed by Mansart in 1685) of coloured marble, which constitutes one of the park's most beautiful ornaments. It is possible to rent bicycles and boats (45F per hr) near the Grand Canal. The Grandes Eaux (when you can see the fountains play) take place on Sun. at 1115 and 1530 May-Oct., at a cost of 15F.

**Le Grand Trianon** 0945-1200, 1400-1700 Tue.-Sun.; 16F, 8F.
A small pink marble-and-stone castle built for Louis XIV by Mansart. This is where the king entertained his intimate friends, Madame de Maintenon in particular. Do not miss the gallery which displays some illustrations of the gardens of Versailles and Trianon.

**Le Petit Trianon** 1400-1700 Tue.-Sun.; 11F, 6F.
A great favourite of Marie-Antoinette's. Its most interesting feature is the Guibert panelling throughout the first-floor apartments. The gardens are in Anglo-Chinese style and lead to the Hameau – ten thatched cottages where the queen liked to indulge her rustic fantasies.

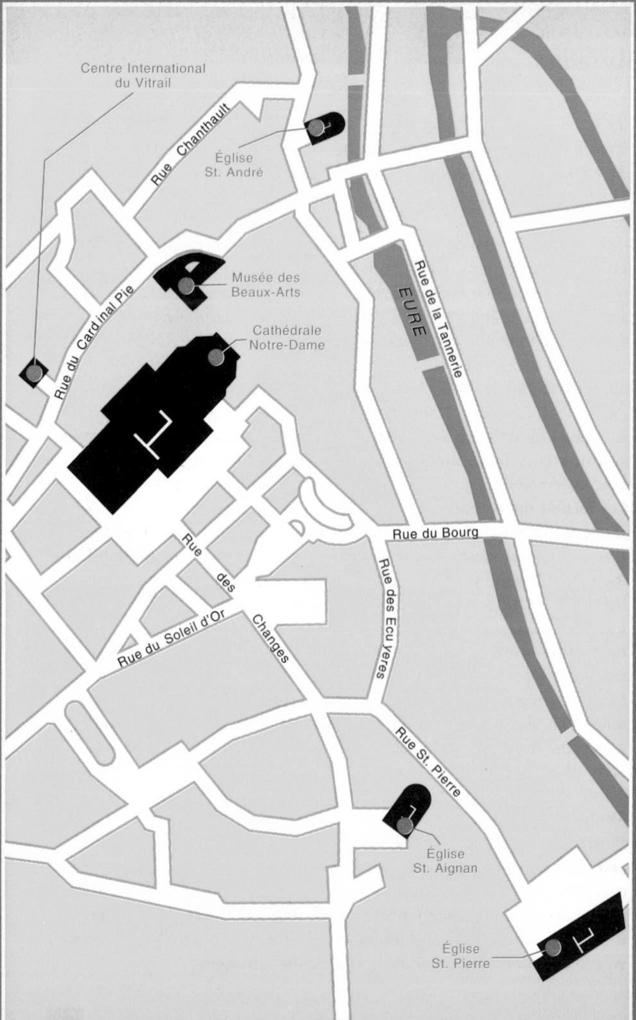

Centre International du Vitrail
Rue Chanthault
Église St. André
Musée des Beaux-Arts
Rue du Cardinal Pie
Cathédrale Notre-Dame
EURE
Rue de la Tannerie
Rue du Bourg
Rue des Changes
Rue des Ecuyeres
Rue du Soleil d'Or
Rue St. Pierre
Église St. Aignan
Église St. Pierre

# Chartres

*90 km south of Paris.*
*SNCF: Montparnasse. Car: A 10 (Paris–Bordeaux) and A 11 (Paris–Le Mans), or RN 10 (Paris–Hendaye).*

Although Chartres is best known for its cathedral it also has many other buildings of historical and architectural interest, and is a charming day out from Paris. Easily accessible by train, from the station follow the signs towards the town centre, keeping the cathedral's twin towers in view. The friendly staff of the Tourist Office in pl. de la Cathédrale (0930-1230, 1400-1830 Mon.-Sat.; 1000-1200, 1500-1800 Sun. in summer) will help you plan your day. You can hire a walkman with two headphones for 35F which takes you through an hour-long self-guided tour of the old town. Otherwise, you can simply follow the signs marked 'Circuit Touristique'. An alternative is a trip on the small tourist train which leaves from pl. de la Cathédrale every 35-40 min (1000-1900 April-Nov.; 25F, child 15F). Buildings of interest include:
**Cathédrale Notre-Dame** 0730-1900; free. This magnificent 13thC High Gothic building dominates the whole town. Erected on the site of an 11thC crypt, it has been a popular place of pilgrimage since the Middle Ages. It is of elegant and majestic dimensions and boasts a unique collection of stained-glass windows covering several centuries and various themes. The treasury (1000-1200, 1400-1800 summer; 1000-1200, 1400-1600 winter) houses the veil of the Virgin Mary donated by Charles the Bald in AD 876. The exterior, with its green copper roof (which replaced the original structure after a fire in 1836), bears two asymmetric towers – the old bell tower (south) and the intricately worked new bell tower (north). Guided tours in English are available at 1215 daily or contact Mr Malcolm Miller (26 rue des Ecuyers, tel: 37281558) to book group tours (400F per hr).
**Centre International du Vitrail** 1000-1230, 1330-1800; 15F, 12F. It is less well known that Chartres is an international stained-glass centre and has over 2500 sq. m of windows throughout its churches. Housed in a fine half-timbered medieval corn loft, the International Centre of Stained-Glass Art runs exhibitions of contemporary artists from all over the world. Underground is the beautiful rib-vaulted, triple-naved Cellier de Loens which is used for social functions.

Crêperie
Les Trois Lys

**Musée des Beaux-Arts** 1000-1200, 1400-1800 Wed.-Mon. in summer, till 1700 in winter; 6F. The museum contains 16th and 18thC tapestries, an important collection of medieval polychrome wood sculptures, 16th-19thC paintings and some interesting harpsichords and spinets. It is housed in the former bishop's beautiful palace, the construction of which spanned four centuries (15th-18th). There is a stunning view over the old town and down to the river Eure from the terraced gardens.

**Eglise St. Pierre.** Founded in the 7thC, it served as the abbey church for the Benedictine monks. The interior is extremely simple and enhanced by the splendour of its late-13th/early-14thC stained-glass windows which occupy the whole of the upper floor.

**Eglise St. André.** On the banks of the river Eure, this former 12thC Romanesque church was restored in 1960 after being partially destroyed by a fire in 1944. The choir used to be on an arch, the remains of which can still be seen, across the river. Today the church is used for video shows and lectures on local history.

**Eglise St. Aignan**. Rebuilt in the 16thC after being damaged by fire, the church shows features of the Renaissance style, especially in the elaborate stained-glass windows of the south side.

**CHÂTEAU DE RAMBOUILLET** 45 km southwest of Paris.
SNCF: Montparnasse. Car: N 10, or A 13, 12 and N 10, or A 10 and N 10. ■ 1000-1200, 1400-1800 Wed.-Mon. ● 25F, child 8F.

The castle of Rambouillet is set in the heart of 20,000 hectares of woodland called the Yvelines forest. It was almost completely rebuilt in the 18thC in medieval style, and all that is left of the original 14thC structure is the round tower of the keep. Once used by numerous kings of France as a hunting residence, it still serves as an official residence of the president. You can visit the charming boudoir of Marie-Antoinette and the private quarters of Napoleon I (see **A-Z**). In the grounds, the exterior of a seemingly simple thatched building belies an interior elaborately decorated in shells, marble and mother-of-pearl. King Louis XVI's present to Marie-Antoinette, an exquisite little dairy, can also be visited.

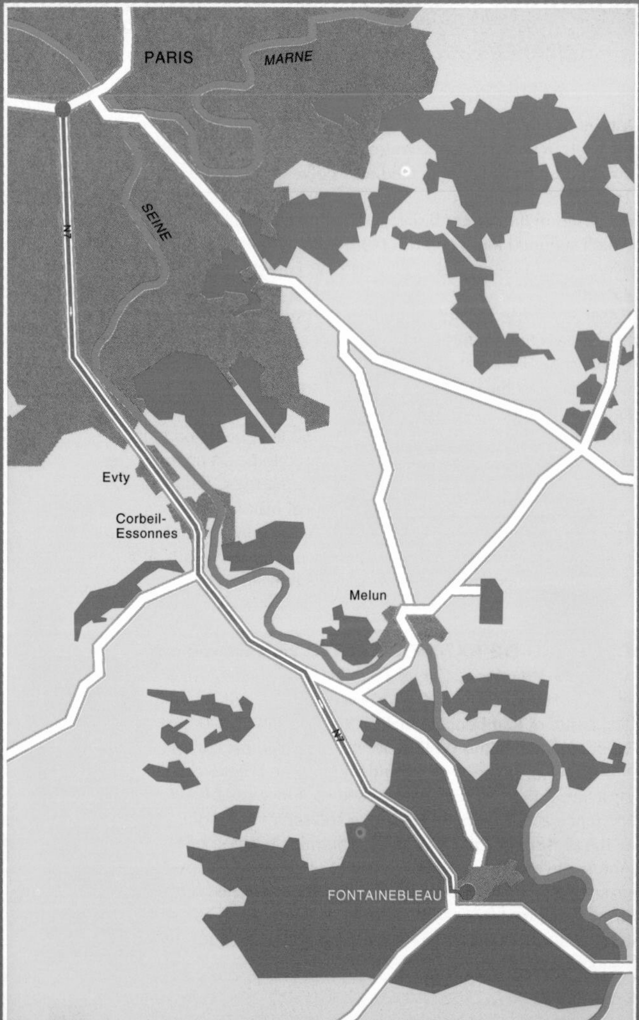
PARIS
MARNE
SEINE
N7
Evty
Corbeil-
Essonnes
Melun
N7
FONTAINEBLEAU

## Fontainebleau

*65 km from Paris.*
*SNCF: Gare de Lyon then bus from Fontainebleau station. Car: N 7 from Porte d'Italie.*

Fontainebleau is a favourite weekend retreat for Parisians attracted by the 20,000 hectare forest and 16thC castle. Visits to the forest are unfortunately limited to those who have their own cars, though it is possible to hire bicycles at the station (40F per day, 30F per half day). If you enjoy walking, maps of suggested itineraries can be obtained from the Tourist Office at 31 pl. Napoléon Bonaparte, opposite the post office.
**Château de Fontainebleau** 0930-1230, 1400-1700 Wed.-Mon. Grands Appartements and Musée Napoléon I; 25F, 18-25 and OAP 13F; Petits Appartements 11F.
Although it dates back to the 12thC, it was François I who was responsible for the castle as it is today, with its ensemble of 16thC buildings and collection of Italian Renaissance art. As you enter the grounds into the Cour des Adieux, where Napoleon I (see **A-Z**) bade farewell to his Imperial Guard after his abdication in 1814, you will see the well-known horseshoe staircase in front of you (Ducerceau, 1634). This leads to the former entrance of the medieval castle on the first floor. A stroll round the Grands Appartements (about 45 min) takes you through the gallery of François I, where you can admire the delicate frescoes by Le Rosso, before going up the Escalier d'Honneur into the splendid ballroom decorated with frescoes by dell'Abbate.
Other rooms on the first floor include the apartments of Madame de Maintenon, Marie-Antoinette and those of Napoleon I, which overlook the Jardins de Diane. Of particular interest are the regal Throne Room, which was the only one existing outside Versailles, and the beautiful Salle du Conseil, which is a fine example of 18thC décor. In the Chapelle de la Trinité are paintings by Freminet. The Petits Appartements (guided tour only) reveal Louis Quinze-style decoration and Empire furniture, and the Galerie des Cerfs with wall paintings depicting royal hunts. To the right of the Cour des Adieux, a passage leads to the Cour de la Fontaine, bordered by a pond filled with carp, some of which are enormous. Go through the Porte Dorée (Golden Gate) to the square terrace for a superb view of the grounds.

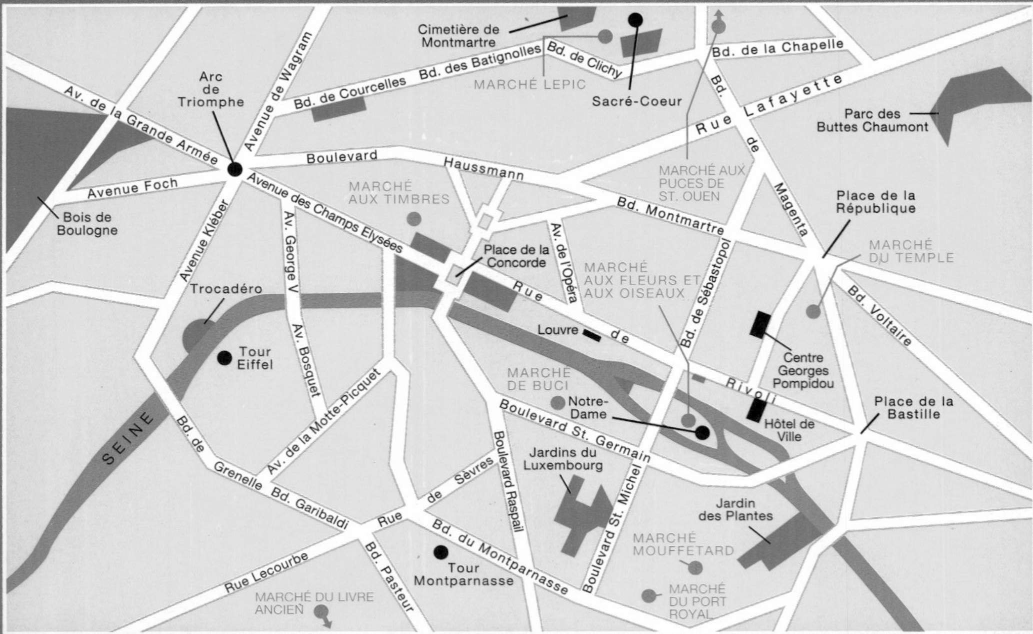
Cimetière de Montmartre
Bd. de Courcelles
Bd. des Batignolles
Bd. de Clichy
MARCHÉ LEPIC
Sacré-Coeur
Bd. de la Chapelle
Rue Lafayette
Parc des Buttes Chaumont
Arc de Triomphe
Av. de la Grande Armée
Avenue de Wagram
Boulevard Haussmann
Avenue Foch
Bois de Boulogne
Avenue Kléber
Avenue des Champs Elysées
MARCHÉ AUX TIMBRES
MARCHÉ AUX PUCES DE ST. OUEN
Bd. de Magenta
Bd. Montmartre
Place de la République
MARCHÉ DU TEMPLE
Place de la Concorde
Av. de l'Opéra
MARCHÉ AUX FLEURS ET AUX OISEAUX
Bd. de Sébastopol
Av. George V
Trocadéro
Tour Eiffel
Av. Bosquet
Rue de Rivoli
Louvre
Centre Georges Pompidou
Bd. Voltaire
MARCHÉ DE BUCI
Notre-Dame
Hôtel de Ville
Place de la Bastille
Boulevard St. Germain
SEINE
Av. de la Motte-Picquet
Bd. de Grenelle
Bd. Garibaldi
Rue de Sèvres
Boulevard Raspail
Jardins du Luxembourg
Boulevard St. Michel
Jardin des Plantes
MARCHÉ MOUFFETARD
Bd. du Montparnasse
Tour Montparnasse
Bd. Pasteur
Rue Lecourbe
MARCHÉ DU LIVRE ANCIEN
MARCHÉ DU PORT ROYAL

**MARCHÉ AUX FLEURS ET AUX OISEAUX** Pl. Louis Lépine, 4e. ■ 0900-1900 Sun.; flowers all week. M Cité.
*Bird and flower market, well worth a visit.*

**MARCHÉ AUX PUCES DE ST. OUEN** Porte de Clignancourt. ■ 0900-2000 Sat.-Mon. M Porte de St. Ouen, Porte de Clignancourt.
*Eight separate markets, each with its own specialities and reputation.*

**MARCHÉ DU LIVRE ANCIEN** Pavillon de Baltard, Parc Georges Brassens, 15e. ■ 0900-1800 Sat. & Sun. M Porte de Vanves.
*This second-hand book market, unique in Paris, is situated at the old Vaugirard horse market.*

**MARCHÉ DE BUCI** Rue de Buci, 6e.
■ 0800-1800 Tue.-Sun. M Odéon.
*Bustling food and flower market.*

**MARCHÉ AUX TIMBRES** Av. Matignon and av. Gabriel, 8e.
■ 1000-dusk Thu., Sat. & Sun. M Franklin D. Roosevelt.
*Stamp and postcard market – a mecca for enthusiasts.* *See* **WALK 4**.

**MARCHÉ DU PORT ROYAL** Bd. de Port Royal, 5e.
■ 0700-1300 Tue., Thu. & Sat. M Port Royal.
*An open-air food market, just one of the 57 markets in Paris.*

**MARCHÉ MOUFFETARD** Rue Mouffetard, 5e.
■ 0830-1900 Tue.-Sun. M Censier Daubenton.
*Typical Parisian food market, colourful with intriguing aromas.* *See* **A-Z**.

**MARCHÉ LEPIC** Rue Lepic, 18e.
■ 0800-1400 Tue.-Sun. M Blanche.
*Food market renowned for its fresh produce.*

**MARCHÉ DU TEMPLE** Rue Perrée, 3e.
■ 0900-1200 Tue.-Sun. M Temple.
*The Carreau du Temple is an old covered market selling mainly clothes.*

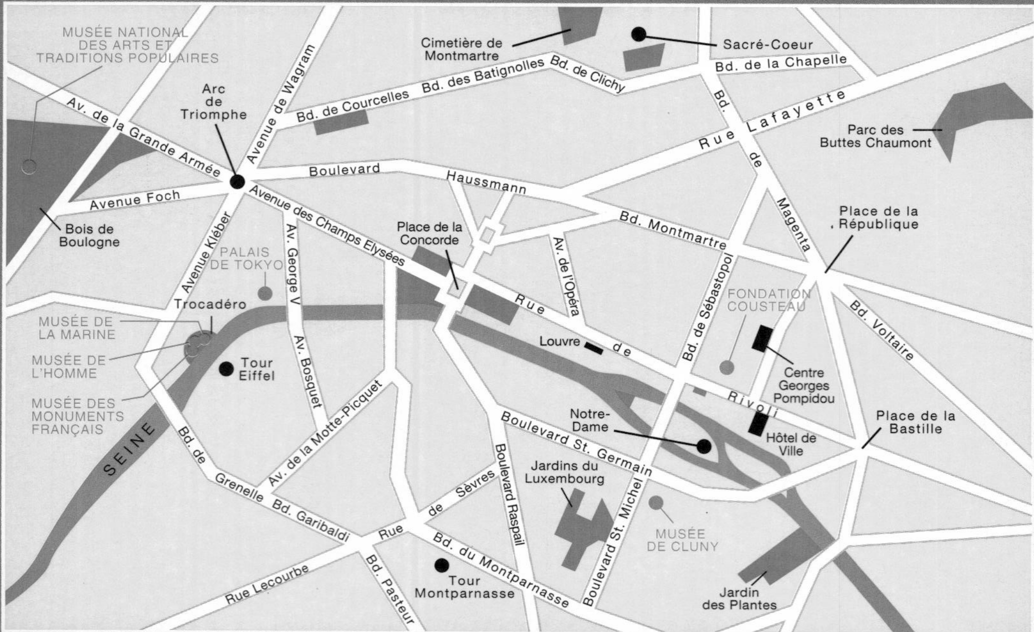
MUSÉE NATIONAL DES ARTS ET TRADITIONS POPULAIRES
Cimetière de Montmartre
Sacré-Coeur
Bd. de la Chapelle
Bd. des Batignolles
Bd. de Clichy
Bd. de Courcelles
Av. de la Grande Armée
Arc de Triomphe
Avenue de Wagram
Parc des Buttes Chaumont
Rue Lafayette
Bd. de Magenta
Boulevard Haussmann
Avenue Foch
Bois de Boulogne
Avenue Kléber
Avenue des Champs Elysées
Place de la Concorde
Bd. Montmartre
Place de la République
PALAIS DE TOKYO
Av. George V
Av. de l'Opéra
Bd. de Sébastopol
FONDATION COUSTEAU
Bd. Voltaire
Trocadéro
Rue de Rivoli
MUSÉE DE LA MARINE
Louvre
MUSÉE DE L'HOMME
Tour Eiffel
Av. Bosquet
Centre Georges Pompidou
MUSÉE DES MONUMENTS FRANÇAIS
Av. de la Motte-Picquet
Notre-Dame
Place de la Bastille
Boulevard St. Germain
Hôtel de Ville
SEINE
Bd. de Grenelle
Jardins du Luxembourg
Rue de Sèvres
Boulevard Raspail
Boulevard St. Michel
Bd. Garibaldi
MUSÉE DE CLUNY
Bd. du Montparnasse
Tour Montparnasse
Rue Lecourbe
Bd. Pasteur
Jardin des Plantes

**PALAIS DE TOKYO** 13 av. du Président Wilson, 16e.
■ 0945-1715 Wed.-Mon. M Iéna. ● 25F.
*The national photography centre, with exhibitions of both historical and contemporary photographs.*

**MUSÉE DE CLUNY** 6 pl. Paul Painlevé, 5e.
■ 0930-1715 Wed.-Mon. M Odéon. ● 15F.
*Medieval arts and crafts, including the* Lady with the Unicorn *tapestry.*

**FONDATION COUSTEAU** Forum des Halles, 1er.
■ 1000-1730. RER Châtelet-Les Halles. ● 75F.
*Displays on deep-sea diving, plus a wreck and 'algae forest' to explore.*

**MUSÉE NATIONAL DES ARTS ET TRADITIONS POPULAIRES** 6 av. du Mahatma Ghandi, 16e.
■ 1000-1715 Wed.-Mon. M Sablons. ● 15F.
*Folk museum depicting everyday life in pre-industrial France according to the theories of Lévi-Strauss. The first part shows the techniques and crafts used by man to survive in his environment and the second illustrates his social and spiritual life.*

**MUSÉE DES MONUMENTS FRANÇAIS** Palais de Chaillot, pl. du Trocadéro, 16e.
■ 0900-1800 Wed.-Mon. M Trocadéro. ● 16F (8F Sun.).
*Based on an idea of Viollet-le-Duc, it displays copies of the most important sculptures, frescoes and murals in France (pre-Roman to 19thC).*

**MUSÉE DE LA MARINE** Palais de Chaillot, pl. du Trocadéro, 16e.
■ 1000-1800 Wed.-Mon. M Trocadéro. ● 18F.
*A superb collection of rare model ships, paintings and engravings.*

**MUSÉE DE L'HOMME** Palais de Chaillot, pl. du Trocadéro, 16e.
■ 0945-1715 Wed.-Mon. M Trocadéro. ● 25F (special exhibitions 16F, or 25F for both).
*Biological, anthropological and historical displays exploring the origins, development and progress of various cultures worldwide.*

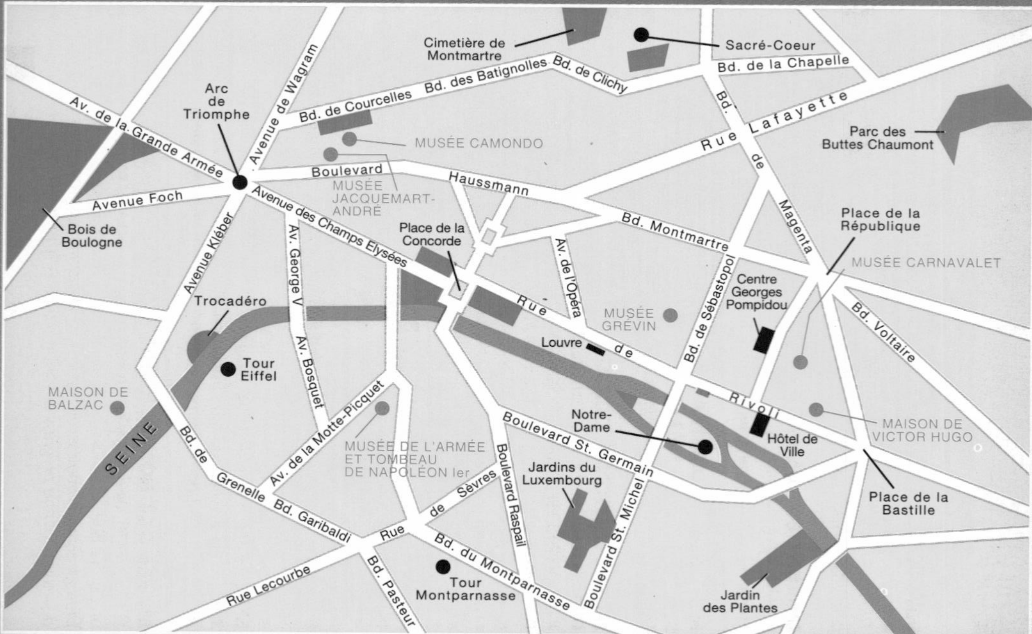
Cimetière de Montmartre
Sacré-Coeur
Bd. de la Chapelle
Bd. des Batignolles
Bd. de Clichy
Bd. de Courcelles
Arc de Triomphe
Avenue de Wagram
Av. de la Grande Armée
Parc des Buttes Chaumont
Rue Lafayette
Bd. de Magenta
MUSÉE CAMONDO
Boulevard Haussmann
MUSÉE JACQUEMART-ANDRÉ
Avenue Foch
Bois de Boulogne
Avenue Kléber
Avenue des Champs Elysées
Place de la Concorde
Bd. Montmartre
Place de la République
MUSÉE CARNAVALET
Av. George V
Av. de l'Opéra
Centre Georges Pompidou
Trocadéro
Rue de Rivoli
MUSÉE GRÉVIN
Bd. de Sébastopol
Bd. Voltaire
Louvre
Tour Eiffel
Av. Bosquet
MAISON DE BALZAC
Av. de la Motte-Picquet
Notre-Dame
Hôtel de Ville
MAISON DE VICTOR HUGO
SEINE
Boulevard St. Germain
Bd. de Grenelle
MUSÉE DE L'ARMÉE ET TOMBEAU DE NAPOLÉON Ier
Boulevard Raspail
Jardins du Luxembourg
Place de la Bastille
Rue de Sèvres
Bd. Garibaldi
Boulevard St. Michel
Bd. du Montparnasse
Tour Montparnasse
Rue Lecourbe
Bd. Pasteur
Jardin des Plantes

**MAISON DE VICTOR HUGO** 6 pl. des Vosges, 4e.
■ 1000-1740 Tue.-Sun. M St. Paul, Chemin Vert. ● 12F.
*16thC residence displaying collections of the 19thC writer Hugo's personal souvenirs, books and illustrations of his works. See* **WALK 2.**

**MAISON DE BALZAC** 47 rue Ràynouard, 16e.
■ 1000-1740 Tue.-Sun. M Passy. ● 15F.
*The home of the great novelist Honoré de Balzac from 1840-47.*

**MUSÉE CARNAVALET** 23 rue de Sévigné, 3e.
■ 1000-1740 Tue.-Sun. M St. Paul. ● 15F.
*Splendid 16th and 17thC mansions (Hôtel de Carnavalet and Hôtel de St. Fargeau) housing exhibits reflecting the history of Paris. See* **WALK 2.**

**MUSÉE JACQUEMART-ANDRÉ** 158 bd. Haussmann, 8e.
■ 1100-1800 Wed.-Sun. M St. Philippe-du-Roule. ● 25F.
*First-rate collection of English, French, northern European and Italian paintings, together with numerous sculptures and pieces of furniture, in a beautiful 19thC house.*

**MUSÉE CAMONDO** 63 rue de Monceau, 8e.
■ 1000-1200, 1400-1700 Wed.-Sun. M Monceau, Villiers. ● 15F.
*Built as a replica of a luxurious 18thC private residence and filled with furniture and* objets d'art.

**MUSEE DE L'ARMÉE ET TOMBEAU DE NAPOLÉON Ier**
Hôtel des Invalides, 7e.
■ 1000-1700 Wed.-Mon. M Latour Maubourg. ● 27F.
*Weapons, uniforms and historical relics from antiquity to World War II. According to his wishes, Napoleon (see* **A-Z***) was buried in the crypt of the church with its 100 m-high gilded dome. See* **CHURCHES, Invalides.**

**MUSÉE GRÉVIN** Forum des Halles, 1er.
■ 1300-1900. RER Châtelet-Les Halles. ● 46F, 6-14 32F.
*The characters and atmosphere of turn-of-the-century Paris are re-created in this waxwork museum.*

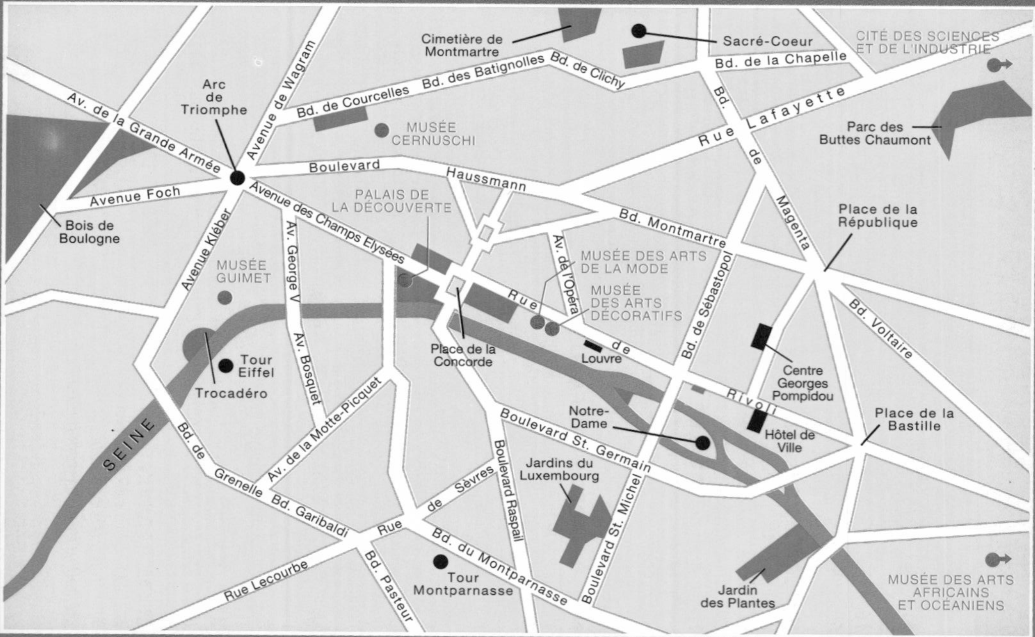

Cimetière de Montmartre
Sacré-Coeur
Cité des Sciences et de l'Industrie
Bd. de la Chapelle
Bd. de Clichy
Bd. des Batignolles
Bd. de Courcelles
Avenue de Wagram
Arc de Triomphe
Av. de la Grande Armée
Musée Cernuschi
Rue Lafayette
Parc des Buttes Chaumont
Boulevard Haussmann
Avenue Foch
Bois de Boulogne
Avenue des Champs Elysées
Palais de la Découverte
Bd. de Magenta
Place de la République
Bd. Montmartre
Avenue Kléber
Musée Guimet
Av. George V
Av. de l'Opéra
Musée des Arts de la Mode
Musée des Arts Décoratifs
Bd. de Sébastopol
Rue de Rivoli
Bd. Voltaire
Tour Eiffel
Trocadéro
Av. Bosquet
Place de la Concorde
Louvre
Centre Georges Pompidou
Seine
Av. de la Motte-Picquet
Notre-Dame
Hôtel de Ville
Place de la Bastille
Boulevard St. Germain
Bd. de Grenelle
Boulevard Raspail
Jardins du Luxembourg
Rue de Sèvres
Bd. Garibaldi
Boulevard St. Michel
Bd. du Montparnasse
Tour Montparnasse
Bd. Pasteur
Rue Lecourbe
Jardin des Plantes
Musée des Arts Africains et Océaniens

**CITÉ DES SCIENCES ET DE L'INDUSTRIE**
30 av. Corentin Cariou, 19e.
■ 1000-1800 Tue.-Sun. M Porte de la Villette. ● 35F.
*Science and technology showcase, in La Villette park. See* **CHILDREN**.

**MUSÉE DES ARTS DÉCORATIFS** 107 rue de Rivoli, 1er.
■ 1230-1800 Wed.-Sun. M Palais Royal, Tuileries. ● 20F.
*Traces the development of the decorative arts from the Middle Ages to the 20thC. Beautiful collections of china and furniture.*

**MUSÉE DES ARTS AFRICAINS ET OCÉANIENS**
293 av. Daumesnil, 12e.
■ 1000-1720 Mon.-Fri., 1000-1800 Sat. & Sun. M Porte Dorée. ● 24F.
*Arts and crafts from Africa, the Pacific and Australia, plus an enormous tropical aquarium.*

**MUSÉE DES ARTS DE LA MODE** 109 rue de Rivoli, 1er.
■ 1230-1830 Wed.-Sat., 1100-1800 Sun. M Palais Royal, Tuileries.
● 20F.
*Also known as Pavillon de Marsan, this museum traces the history of* haute couture *and displays creations by Chanel, Dior, Yves-Saint Laurent and many other great fashion designers.*

**PALAIS DE LA DÉCOUVERTE** Av. Franklin D. Roosevelt, 8e.
■ 1000-1800 Tue.-Sun. M Franklin D. Roosevelt. ● 20F.
*Fascinating educational exhibits illustrating and explaining some of the great scientific discoveries.*

**MUSÉE CERNUSCHI** 7 av. Velasquez, 8e.
■ 1000-1740 Tue.-Sun. M Villiers. ● 9F.
*Collection of ancient Chinese art, with especially fine chinaware.*

**MUSÉE GUIMET** 6 pl. d'Iéna, 16e.
■ 0945-1715 Wed.-Mon. M Iéna. ● 25F.
*Beautifully displayed selection of Asian and Oriental works of art, including statues and ceramics.*

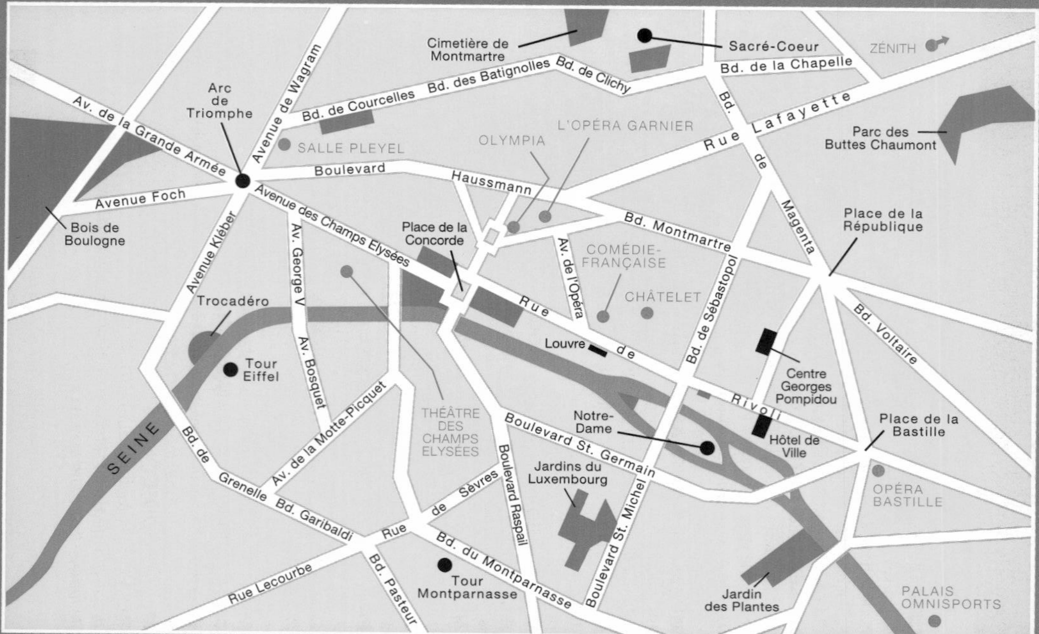

Cimetière de Montmartre
Sacré-Coeur
ZÉNITH
Bd. de la Chapelle
Bd. de Courcelles
Bd. des Batignolles
Bd. de Clichy
Arc de Triomphe
Avenue de Wagram
Av. de la Grande Armée
Bd.
Rue Lafayette
Parc des Buttes Chaumont
SALLE PLEYEL
OLYMPIA
L'OPÉRA GARNIER
Boulevard Haussmann
Avenue Foch
Bois de Boulogne
Avenue des Champs Elysées
Avenue Kléber
Av. George V
Place de la Concorde
Bd. Montmartre
Rue de Magenta
Place de la République
Av. de l'Opéra
COMÉDIE-FRANÇAISE
CHÂTELET
Trocadéro
Rue de Rivoli
Louvre
Bd. de Sébastopol
Bd. Voltaire
Tour Eiffel
Av. Bosquet
Centre Georges Pompidou
SEINE
Av. de la Motte-Picquet
THÉÂTRE DES CHAMPS ELYSÉES
Boulevard St. Germain
Notre-Dame
Hôtel de Ville
Place de la Bastille
Bd. de Grenelle
Bd. Garibaldi
Rue de Sèvres
Boulevard Raspail
Jardins du Luxembourg
Boulevard St. Michel
OPÉRA BASTILLE
Rue Lecourbe
Bd. Pasteur
Tour Montparnasse
Bd. du Montparnasse
Jardin des Plantes
PALAIS OMNISPORTS

**L'OPÉRA GARNIER** Pl. de l'Opéra, 9e.
■ Box office 1100-2000, visits 1100-1700. M Opéra. ● 300F-600F.
*The world's largest opera house, the Palais Garnier. See* **A-Z**.

**OPÉRA BASTILLE** Pl. de la Bastille, 11e.
■ Box office 1100-1830. ● 40F-520F.
*Varied repertoire of classical and modern productions. See* **Bastille**.

**THÉÂTRE DES CHAMPS ELYSÉES** 15 av. Montaigne, 8e.
■ See programme for times. M Alma Marceau. ● 40F-300F.
*Built 1912; has been played by the Marquis de Cuevas and Louis Jouvet.*

**COMÉDIE-FRANÇAISE** Pl. Colette, 1er.
■ Box office 1100-1900. M Palais Royal. ● 45F-195F.
*The oldest Parisian theatre, built by Richelieu, is the home of the Molière players, whose repertoire goes beyond just the traditional classics.*

**SALLE PLEYEL** 252 rue du Faubourg St. Honoré, 8e.
■ See programme for times. M Ternes. ● 50F-350F.
*Home of the Orchestre de Paris, and a shrine for classical music lovers.*

**CHÂTELET** Pl. du Châtelet, 1er.
■ See programme for times and prices. RER Châtelet-Les Halles.
*Presents light opera, concerts, ballets and a few musical comedies.*

**OLYMPIA** 28 bd. des Capucines, 9e.
■ Box office 1000-1900. M Opéra, Madeleine. ● 100F-220F.
*Most famous music hall in Paris, host to French and international stars.*

**PALAIS OMNISPORTS** 8 bd. de Bercy, 12e.
■ See programme for times and prices. M Bercy, Quai de la Gare.
*Multipurpose venue; hosts opera, rock concerts, cycle races, ice hockey.*

**ZÉNITH** 211 av. Jean Jaurès, 19e.
■ See programme for times and prices. M Porte de Pantin.
*A massive 'inflatable' venue for rock and pop concerts.*

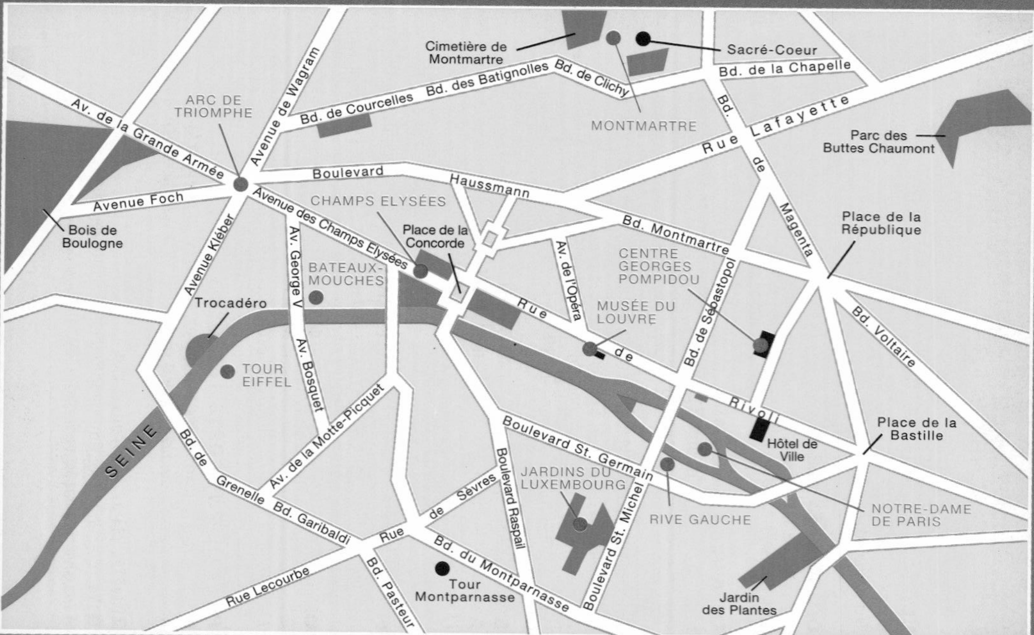

Cimetière de Montmartre
Sacré-Coeur
Bd. de la Chapelle
Bd. de Clichy
Bd. des Batignolles
Bd. de Courcelles
Av. de la Grande Armée
ARC DE TRIOMPHE
Avenue de Wagram
MONTMARTRE
Parc des Buttes Chaumont
Rue Lafayette
Bd. de Magenta
Boulevard Haussmann
Avenue Foch
Bois de Boulogne
Avenue des Champs Elysées
CHAMPS ELYSÉES
Place de la Concorde
Avenue Kléber
Av. George V
BATEAUX-MOUCHES
Trocadéro
Rue de Rivoli
Av. de l'Opéra
Bd. Montmartre
CENTRE GEORGES POMPIDOU
Place de la République
MUSÉE DU LOUVRE
Bd. de Sébastopol
Bd. Voltaire
TOUR EIFFEL
Av. Bosquet
Av. de la Motte-Picquet
SEINE
Boulevard St. Germain
Hôtel de Ville
Place de la Bastille
Bd. de Grenelle
Boulevard Raspail
JARDINS DU LUXEMBOURG
Rue de Sèvres
Bd. Garibaldi
Boulevard St. Michel
RIVE GAUCHE
NOTRE-DAME DE PARIS
Bd. du Montparnasse
Tour Montparnasse
Rue Lecourbe
Bd. Pasteur
Jardin des Plantes

## BATEAUX-MOUCHES
*Glass-topped cruise boats which carry tourists up and down the Seine (see* **A-Z***). Floodlit evening trips are particularly enjoyable. See* **A-Z**.

## CHAMPS ELYSÉES
*Famous avenue, with the Arc de Triomphe (see* **A-Z***) at its western end. Try a coffee at Le Fouquet's (see* **CAFÉS***). See* **WALK 4**, **A-Z**.

## TOUR EIFFEL
*Not to be missed, Gustave Eiffel's world-famous tower with tremendous views over the city. See* **A-Z**.

## LEFT BANK (RIVE GAUCHE)
*Bustling streets with fascinating bookshops, lots of students and cobbled quays by the Seine (see* **A-Z***). See* **CITY DISTRICTS**, **WALK 3**, **A-Z**.

## MUSÉE DU LOUVRE
*Probably the world's most important art collection, including the* Mona Lisa *(see* **A-Z***) and* Venus de Milo. *See* **ART GALLERIES**, **A-Z**.

## MONTMARTRE
*Funicular railway to the top of Montmartre and to Sacré-Coeur (see* **A-Z***), giving incredible views over the city. See* **CITY DISTRICTS**, **WALK 5**, **A-Z**.

## NOTRE-DAME DE PARIS
*The cathedral church of Paris and an outstanding example of French art and architecture. The rose windows, soaring buttresses and west façade are particularly noteworthy. See* **CHURCHES**, **WALK 1**, **A-Z**.

## CENTRE GEORGES POMPIDOU
*Multicultural centre, built to a controversial design. There are excellent street entertainers outside. See* **A-Z**.

## JARDINS DU LUXEMBOURG
*Stroll among the lovers, students studying in the sun, children playing; watch a game of* boules*; sit and watch Paris relaxing. See* **PARKS**, **A-Z**.

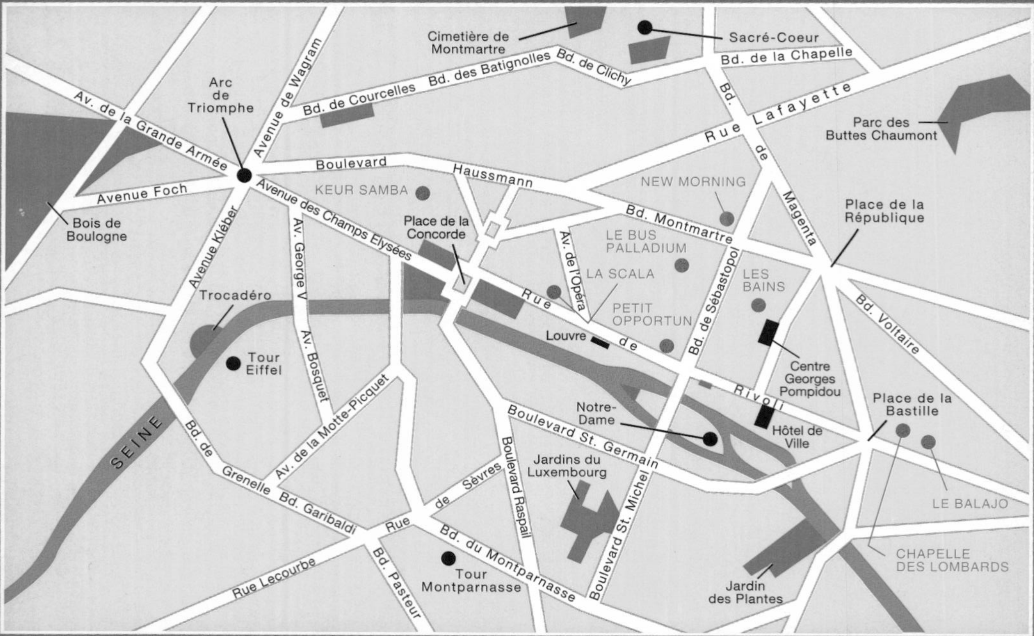
Cimetière de Montmartre
Sacré-Coeur
Bd. de la Chapelle
Bd. de Courcelles
Bd. des Batignolles
Bd. de Clichy
Arc de Triomphe
Av. de la Grande Armée
Avenue de Wagram
Rue Lafayette
Parc des Buttes Chaumont
Bd. de Magenta
Boulevard Haussmann
Avenue Foch
Bois de Boulogne
KEUR SAMBA
NEW MORNING
Avenue des Champs Elysées
Avenue Kléber
Av. George V
Place de la Concorde
Bd. Montmartre
Place de la République
LE BUS PALLADIUM
Av. de l'Opéra
LA SCALA
LES BAINS
Trocadéro
Rue de Rivoli
PETIT OPPORTUN
Bd. de Sébastopol
Bd. Voltaire
Louvre
Tour Eiffel
Av. Bosquet
Centre Georges Pompidou
Place de la Bastille
Notre-Dame
Hôtel de Ville
Boulevard St. Germain
SEINE
Bd. de Grenelle
Av. de la Motte-Picquet
Jardins du Luxembourg
Boulevard Raspail
Rue de Sèvres
LE BALAJO
Bd. Garibaldi
Boulevard St. Michel
Bd. du Montparnasse
Tour Montparnasse
CHAPELLE DES LOMBARDS
Jardin des Plantes
Rue Lecourbe
Bd. Pasteur

**LA CHAPELLE DES LOMBARDS** 19 rue de Lappe, 11e.
■ 2230-dawn Thu.-Sat. M Bastille. ● 100F, inc. first drink.
*Afro-Cuban (zouc), reggae, African and Latin American music in a simple but cosy setting. Mixed crowd.*

**NEW MORNING** 7-9 rue des Petites Ecuries, 9e.
■ 2100-0130. Concerts start 2200. M Château d'Eau. ● Varies.
*Spacious, comfortable venue for big-name jazz bands and musicians.*

**PETIT OPPORTUN** 15 rue des Lavandières Ste Opportune, 1er.
■ 2300-0300 Wed.-Mon. RER Châtelet-Les Halles. ● Varies.
*Great place for well-known jazz musicians, especially Americans.*

**LES BAINS** 7 rue du Bourg-l'Abbé, 3e.
■ 2300-0600. M Etienne Marcel. ● 120F, inc. first drink.
*Extremely trendy nightspot in an old Turkish bathhouse!*

**LA SCALA** 188 rue de Rivoli, 1er.
■ 2230-dawn. M Tuileries, Palais Royal. ● 80F, inc. first drink.
*Very large, with five bars and three dance floors. Popular and crowded.*

**LE BALAJO** 9 rue de Lappe, 11e.
■ 2200-0430 Mon., Fri. & Sat. M Bastille. ● 100F, inc. first drink.
*Varied entertainment, with disco on Mon. and ballroom dancing at the weekend.*

**KEUR SAMBA** 79 rue La Boétie, 8e.
■ 2300-dawn. M Miromesnil, St. Philippe-du-Roule. ● 120F, inc. first drink.
*African, Afro-Cuban and American soul music plus present hits in an exotic setting with painted elephants and carved African heads.*

**LE BUS PALLADIUM** 6 rue Fontaine, 9e.
■ 2300-dawn Tue.-Sun. M St. Georges. ● 110F, inc. first drink.
*This is the 'in' place for students and upwardly-mobiles to compare their cashmere sweaters!*

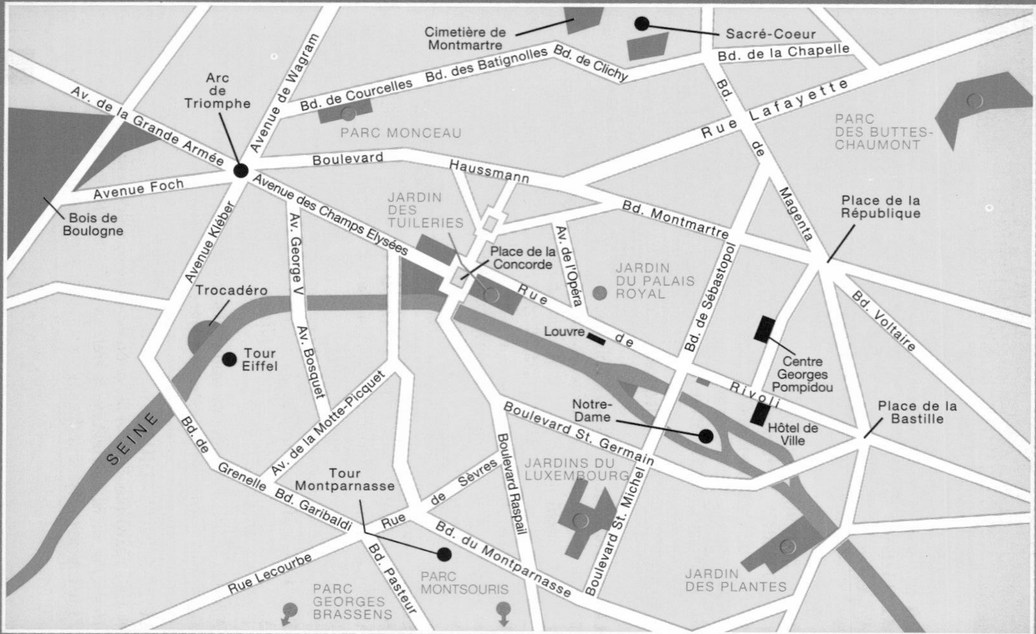

Cimetière de Montmartre
Sacré-Coeur
Bd. de la Chapelle
Bd. des Batignolles
Bd. de Clichy
Bd. de Courcelles
Avenue de Wagram
Arc de Triomphe
Av. de la Grande Armée
PARC MONCEAU
Rue Lafayette
PARC DES BUTTES-CHAUMONT
Boulevard Haussmann
Avenue Foch
Bois de Boulogne
Avenue des Champs Elysées
Avenue Kléber
Av. George V
JARDIN DES TUILERIES
Place de la Concorde
Av. de l'Opéra
Bd. Montmartre
Bd. de Magenta
Place de la République
JARDIN DU PALAIS ROYAL
Bd. de Sébastopol
Rue de Rivoli
Louvre
Trocadéro
Tour Eiffel
Av. Bosquet
Bd. Voltaire
Centre Georges Pompidou
Notre-Dame
Hôtel de Ville
Place de la Bastille
SEINE
Av. de la Motte-Picquet
Boulevard St. Germain
Boulevard Raspail
Bd. de Grenelle
Bd. Garibaldi
Tour Montparnasse
Rue de Sèvres
JARDINS DU LUXEMBOURG
Boulevard St. Michel
Bd. du Montparnasse
Rue Lecourbe
Bd. Pasteur
PARC GEORGES BRASSENS
PARC MONTSOURIS
JARDIN DES PLANTES

**JARDIN DES PLANTES** Rue Cuvier, 5e.
■ 0715-dusk (summer), 0800-dusk (winter). M Jussieu.
● Gardens free; menagerie 25F.
*Extensive botanical gardens with 10,000 different species of plants. There are also a small zoo and natural history museum.*

**JARDIN DES TUILERIES** Rue de Rivoli, 1er.
■ 0800-2000. M Tuileries, Concorde. ● Free.
*Gardens designed by the notable landscape gardener Le Nôtre, on the right bank of the Seine (see* **A-Z**).

**JARDINS DU LUXEMBOURG** Bd. St. Michel, 6e.
■ 0730-dusk. RER Luxembourg. ● Free.
*Gardens of the Senate House, with tennis, croquet, children's playground, café, fountains, formal vistas and sunbathers. See* **A-Z**.

**JARDIN DU PALAIS ROYAL** Pl. du Palais Royal, 1er.
■ 24 hr. M Palais Royal. ● Free.
*Formal gardens lined by arcades, with a modern sculpture by Buren.*

**PARC DES BUTTES-CHAUMONT** Rue Manin and rue de Crimée, 19e.
■ 0700-2300. M Buttes-Chaumont, Botzaris. ● Free.
*Waterfalls, a lake, grottoes and views of Montmartre (see* **A-Z**).

**PARC MONTSOURIS** Bd. Jourdan and rue Gazan, 14e.
■ 0800-dusk. RER Cité Universitaire. ● Free.
*Site of the municipal observatory, with a splendid lake and waterfalls.*

**PARC MONCEAU** Bd. de Courcelles, 8e.
■ 24 hr. M Courcelles, Monceau. ● Free.
*18thC garden with pagodas, follies, a playground and roller-skating park.*

**PARC GEORGES BRASSENS** Rue des Morillons, 15e.
■ 0800-dusk. M Convention. ● Free.
*New garden in centre of the city – try to visit the aromatic herb garden.*

Chez Andre

KLEBER
KLÉBER
CAFÉ
GLACIER

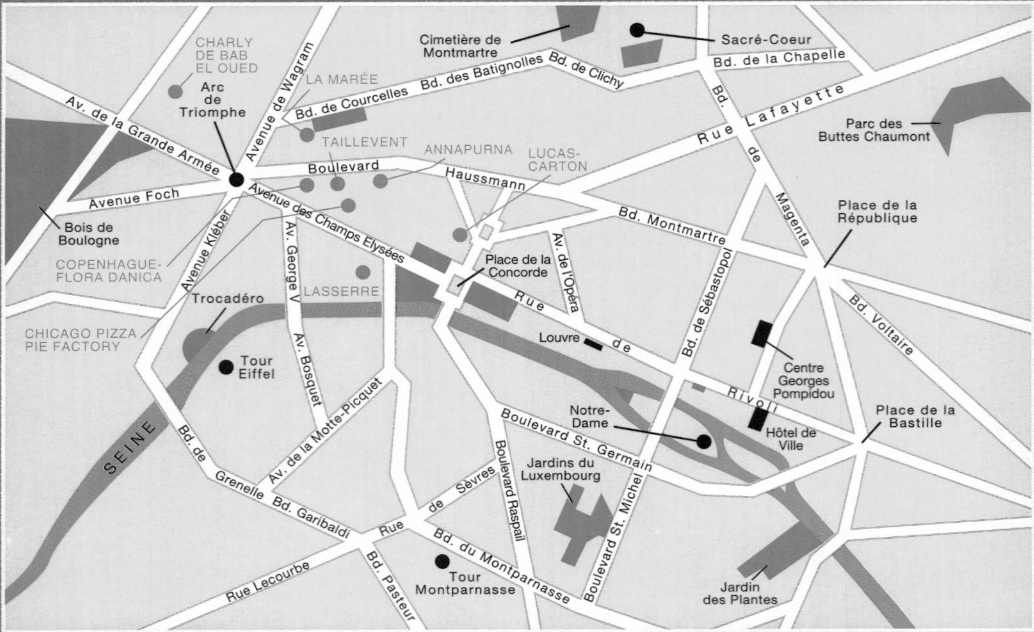
CHARLY
DE BAB
EL OUED
Arc
de
Triomphe
Avenue de Wagram
LA MARÉE
Bd. de Courcelles
Bd. des Batignolles
Bd. de Clichy
Cimetière de
Montmartre
Sacré-Coeur
Bd. de la Chapelle
Bd.
de
Magenta
Rue Lafayette
Parc des
Buttes Chaumont
Av. de la Grande Armée
TAILLEVENT
ANNAPURNA
LUCAS-
CARTON
Boulevard
Haussmann
Avenue Foch
Bois de
Boulogne
Avenue des Champs Elysées
Avenue Kléber
COPENHAGUE-
FLORA DANICA
Av. George V
LASSERRE
Bd. Montmartre
Av. de l'Opéra
Place de la
Concorde
Place de la
République
Bd. de Sébastopol
Bd. Voltaire
Trocadéro
CHICAGO PIZZA
PIE FACTORY
Tour
Eiffel
Av. Bosquet
Rue de Rivoli
Louvre
Centre
Georges
Pompidou
Hôtel de
Ville
Place de la
Bastille
Notre-
Dame
SEINE
Bd. de Grenelle
Av. de la Motte-Picquet
Boulevard St. Germain
Boulevard Raspail
Jardins du
Luxembourg
Boulevard St. Michel
Rue de Sèvres
Bd. Garibaldi
Bd. du Montparnasse
Tour
Montparnasse
Rue Lecourbe
Bd. Pasteur
Jardin
des Plantes

**LUCAS-CARTON** 9 pl. de la Madeleine, 8e.
■ Till 2230 Mon.-Fri. Closed Aug. M Madeleine. ● 500F-1000F.
*Voted best in Paris, 1988. Excellent cuisine in Art Deco surroundings.*

**TAILLEVENT** 15 rue Lammenais, 8e.
■ Till 2200 Mon.-Fri. Closed mid July-mid Aug. M George V.
● 650F, inc. wine.
*Prestigious restaurant, much admired for its* nouvelle cuisine.

**LA MARÉE** 1 rue Daru, 8e.
■ 1230-1430, 2000-2230 Mon.-Fri. M Ternes, Courcelles. ● 600F.
*Excellent fresh seafood, simply cooked and professionally served.*

**COPENHAGUE-FLORA DANICA** 142 av. des Champs Elysées, 8e. ■ 1200-1430, 1915-2230. Closed Sun. & Aug. (Copenhague).
M Etoile, George V. RER Charles-de-Gaulle. ● 200F-300F.
*Copenhague is on the first floor, the cheaper Flora Danica plus snack bar on the ground floor.*

**ANNAPURNA** 32 rue de Berri, 8e.
■ Till 2330. Closed Sat. lunch & Sun. M St. Philippe-du-Roule. ● 200F.
*Much respected Indian restaurant, the oldest in the city.*

**CHARLY DE BAB EL OUED** 95 bd. Gouvion-St. Cyr, 17e.
■ 1200-1415, 2000-2215. M Porte Maillot. Reservation recommended.
● 200F.
*Authentic Middle Eastern food served amid palms and pot plants.*

**LASSERRE** 17 av. Franklin D. Roosevelt, 8e.
■ Till 2230. Closed Sun., Mon. lunch & Aug. M Franklin D. Roosevelt.
● 700F.
*World-famous; opened just after the war and retains the original décor.*

**CHICAGO PIZZA PIE FACTORY** 5 rue de Berri, 8e.
■ 1145-0100. M George V. ● 100F.
*Authentic 'deep-dish' pizzas. Happy hour is 1800-1930; cocktails.*

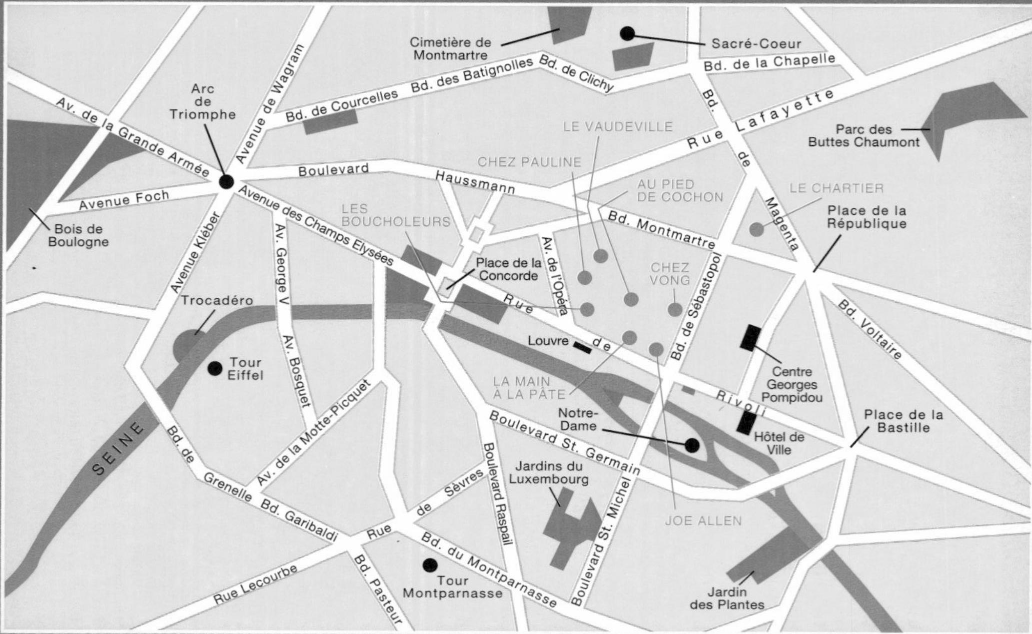
Cimetière de Montmartre
Sacré-Coeur
Bd. de la Chapelle
Bd. de Courcelles
Bd. des Batignolles
Bd. de Clichy
Arc de Triomphe
Avenue de Wagram
Av. de la Grande Armée
Bd. Lafayette
Rue de Magenta
Parc des Buttes Chaumont
LE VAUDEVILLE
CHEZ PAULINE
Boulevard Haussmann
AU PIED DE COCHON
LE CHARTIER
Place de la République
Avenue Foch
Bois de Boulogne
Avenue Kléber
Avenue des Champs Elysées
LES BOUCHOLEURS
Av. George V
Place de la Concorde
Av. de l'Opéra
Bd. Montmartre
CHEZ VONG
Trocadéro
Rue de Rivoli
Louvre
Bd. de Sébastopol
Bd. Voltaire
Tour Eiffel
Av. Bosquet
LA MAIN À LA PÂTE
Centre Georges Pompidou
Av. de la Motte-Picquet
Notre-Dame
Hôtel de Ville
Place de la Bastille
SEINE
Boulevard St. Germain
Bd. de Grenelle
Boulevard Raspail
Jardins du Luxembourg
Rue de Sèvres
Bd. Garibaldi
Boulevard St. Michel
JOE ALLEN
Bd. du Montparnasse
Tour Montparnasse
Rue Lecourbe
Bd. Pasteur
Jardin des Plantes

**CHEZ PAULINE** 5 rue Villedo, 1er.
■ 1215-1430, 1930-2230. Closed Sat. eve, Sun. & July. M Pyramides.
● 400F.
*Traditional French cuisine served in a classical and comfortable setting; popular with the locals as well as tourists. Good wines.*

**CHEZ VONG** 10 rue de la Grande Truanderie, 1er.
■ 1200-1400, 1900-2400 Mon.-Sat. M Etienne Marcel. ● 200F-300F.
*One of the best Chinese restaurants in Paris with refined cooking and an elegant setting.*

**LE VAUDEVILLE** 39 rue Vivienne, 2e.
■ Till 0200. M Bourse. ● 200F-300F.
*Seafood restaurant with 30s décor frequented by Bourse financiers for lunch, and journalists and theatregoers in the evening.*

**LA MAIN À LA PÂTE** 35 rue St. Honoré, 1er.
■ 1130-0300 Mon.-Sat. RER Châtelet-Les Halles. ● 250F, inc. wine.
*Adjacent to Forum des Halles; very friendly, cheerful atmosphere.*

**AU PIED DE COCHON** 6 rue Coquillière, 1er.
■ 24 hr. RER Châtelet-Les Halles. ● 250F.
*In the 'Les Halles' tradition with 19thC interior and seafood specialities.*

**LES BOUCHOLEURS** 4 rue de Richelieu, 1er.
■ 1200-1400, 1930-2200. Closed Sat. lunch & Sun. M Palais Royal.
● 200F.
*Small restaurant with a nautical interior. Specializes in seafood.*

**JOE ALLEN** 30 rue Pierre Lescot, 1er.
■ 1200-0200. M Etienne Marcel. ● 150F-200F.
*Popular New York-style eatery serving barbecue ribs and cheesecake.*

**LE CHARTIER** 7 rue du Faubourg Montmartre, 9e.
■ 1100-1500, 1800-2130. M Rue Montmartre. ● 60F.
*Poor man's Maxim's. Superb* fin de siècle *setting. Traditional cooking.*

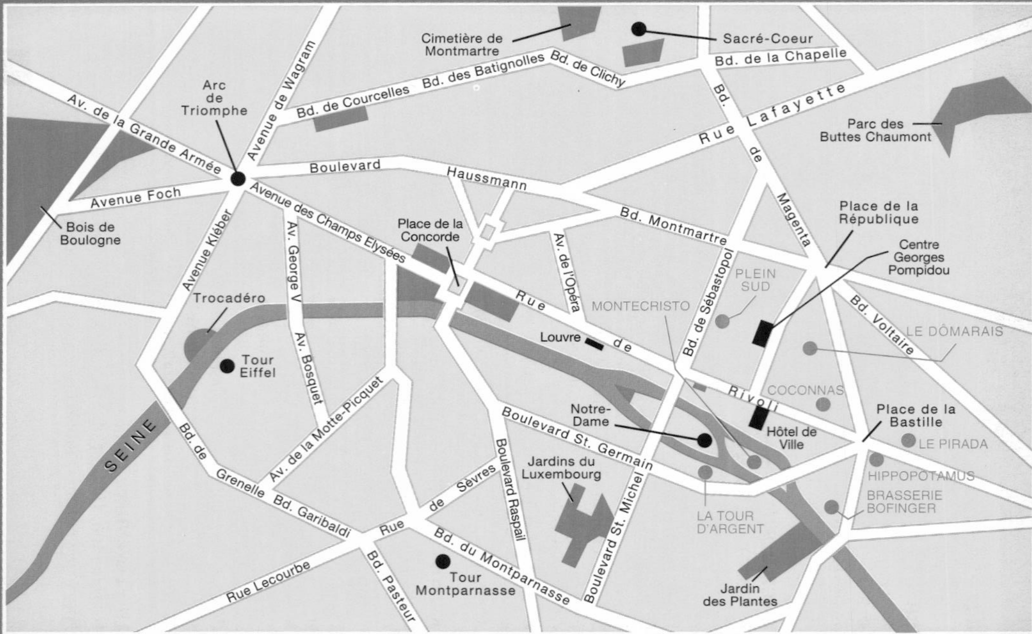
Cimetière de Montmartre
Sacré-Coeur
Bd. de la Chapelle
Bd. de Clichy
Bd. des Batignolles
Bd. de Courcelles
Arc de Triomphe
Avenue de Wagram
Av. de la Grande Armée
Rue Lafayette
Parc des Buttes Chaumont
Bd. de Magenta
Boulevard Haussmann
Avenue Foch
Bois de Boulogne
Avenue des Champs Elysées
Place de la Concorde
Bd. Montmartre
Place de la République
Centre Georges Pompidou
Av. George V
Av. de l'Opéra
Bd. de Sébastopol
PLEIN SUD
Avenue Kléber
Trocadéro
Rue de Rivoli
MONTECRISTO
Bd. Voltaire
LE DÔMARAIS
Louvre
Tour Eiffel
Av. Bosquet
COCONNAS
Place de la Bastille
Notre-Dame
Hôtel de Ville
LE PIRADA
SEINE
Bd. de Grenelle
Av. de la Motte-Picquet
Boulevard St. Germain
Boulevard Raspail
Jardins du Luxembourg
HIPPOPOTAMUS
BRASSERIE BOFINGER
Rue de Sèvres
Bd. Garibaldi
LA TOUR D'ARGENT
Bd. du Montparnasse
Boulevard St. Michel
Bd. Pasteur
Tour Montparnasse
Rue Lecourbe
Jardin des Plantes

**LA TOUR D'ARGENT** 17 quai de la Tournelle, 5e.
■ 1200-1400, 2000-2200 Tue.-Sun. M Maubert-Mutualité.
● 500F (lunch 350F).
*Excellent food, and great views of Notre-Dame de Paris (see* **A-Z***).*

**LE DÔMARAIS** 53 bis rue des Francs Bourgeois, 4e.
■ 1130-2330. Closed Mon. lunch, Sat. & Sun. M Hôtel de Ville, Rambuteau. ● 280F.
*In the heart of the Marais; exceptional circular dining room with cupola.*

**BRASSERIE BOFINGER** 3 rue de la Bastille, 4e.
■ 1200-1500, 1930-0100. M Bastille. ● 150F-200F.
*Established in 1864, this is the oldest brasserie in Paris and retains its 1900s décor; try the* choucroute *(sauerkraut).*

**COCONNAS** 2 bis pl. des Vosges, 4e.
■ 1215-1415, 1945-2200 Wed.-Sun. Closed mid Dec.-mid Jan.
M St. Paul. ● 150F-200F.
*Traditional French cuisine in a tavern atmosphere.*

**MONTECRISTO** 81 rue St. Louis-en-l'Île, 4e.
■ 1200-1430, 1800-2400. Closed Aug. M Pont Marie. ● 150F-200F.
*An old Île St. Louis house offering friendly service in attractive, small dining rooms.*

**HIPPOPOTAMUS** Pl. de la Bastille, 11e.
■ 1130-0100. M Bastille. ● 150F.
*One of a chain of restaurants specializing in grilled beef dishes.*

**PLEIN SUD** 10 rue St. Merri, 4e.
■ 0730-0030. M Rambuteau, Hôtel de Ville. ● 120F.
*The explosive cocktails and enchiladas are well worth a try.*

**LE PIRADA** 7 rue de Lappe, 11e.
■ 1200-1500, 1900-0200 Mon.-Sat. M Bastille. ● 50F-120F.
*Spanish specialities are served in a lively atmosphere.*

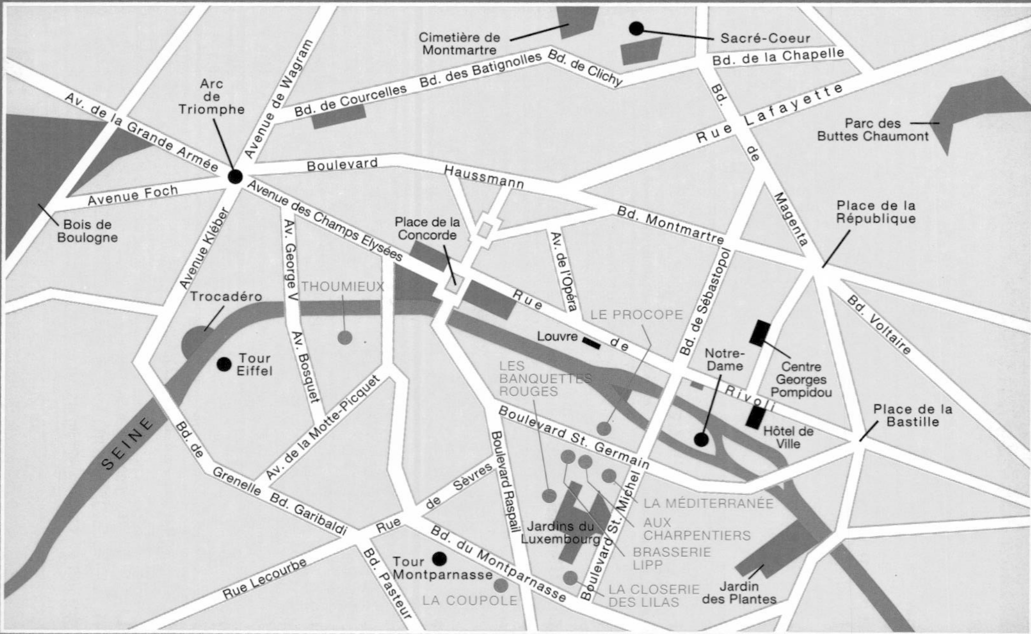

Cimetière de Montmartre
Sacré-Coeur
Bd. de la Chapelle
Bd. des Batignolles
Bd. de Clichy
Bd. de Courcelles
Arc de Triomphe
Avenue de Wagram
Av. de la Grande Armée
Rue Lafayette
Parc des Buttes Chaumont
Bd. de Magenta
Boulevard Haussmann
Avenue Foch
Bois de Boulogne
Avenue Kléber
Avenue des Champs Elysées
Place de la Concorde
Av. de l'Opéra
Bd. Montmartre
Place de la République
Av. George V
THOUMIEUX
Trocadéro
Rue de Rivoli
LE PROCOPE
Bd. de Sébastopol
Bd. Voltaire
Louvre
Tour Eiffel
Av. Bosquet
Notre-Dame
Centre Georges Pompidou
LES BANQUETTES ROUGES
Place de la Bastille
Hôtel de Ville
Av. de la Motte-Picquet
SEINE
Bd. de Grenelle
Boulevard St. Germain
Boulevard Raspail
Rue de Sèvres
Bd. Garibaldi
LA MÉDITERRANÉE
Jardins du Luxembourg
AUX CHARPENTIERS
Boulevard St. Michel
BRASSERIE LIPP
Tour Montparnasse
Bd. du Montparnasse
Rue Lecourbe
Bd. Pasteur
LA CLOSERIE DES LILAS
Jardin des Plantes
LA COUPOLE

**LA CLOSERIE DES LILAS** 171 bd. du Montparnasse, 6e.
■ Till 0100. M Port Royal. ● 300F.
*Two restaurants, terrace and piano bar. Popular with showbiz and literary people. See* **Montparnasse**.

**LA MÉDITERRANÉE** 2 pl. de l'Odéon, 6e.
■ 1200-1500, 1900-2300. M Odéon/RER Luxembourg. ● 195F-300F.
*Meeting place for writers and artists in the 50s, including Cocteau.*

**BRASSERIE LIPP** 151 bd. St. Germain, 6e.
■ 1200-0200. Closed 23 Dec.-2 Jan. M St. Germain-des-Prés.
● 200F-300F.
*Mingle with the journalists, writers and politicians who congregate in this world-famous restaurant.*

**LA COUPOLE** 102 bd. du Montparnasse, 6e.
■ Till 0200. M Vavin. ● 180F-300F.
*Noisy, crowded Art Deco establishment serving great French fish dishes.*

**AUX CHARPENTIERS** 10 rue Mabillon, 6e.
■ 1200-1500, 1900-2330 Mon.-Sat. Closed 25-31 Dec. M Mabillon.
● 220F.
*Traditional French cooking served in a bistro established in 1856.*

**LES BANQUETTES ROUGES** 28 rue Monsieur Le Prince, 6e.
■ Till 2300 Mon.-Sat. M Odéon. ● 150F-200F.
*At end of a courtyard, meals are served on a terrace in a tranquil setting.*

**THOUMIEUX** 79 rue St. Dominique, 7e.
■ 1200-1500, 1930-2300. M Gaîté. ● 120F-200F.
*Specializes in food from the southwest of France: excellent casseroles.*

**LE PROCOPE** 13 rue de l'Ancienne-Comédie, 6e.
■ 0800-0200. M Odéon. ● À la carte 200F, set menu 70F.
*This is the oldest café in Paris (1670) and a famous rendezvous for intellectuals.*

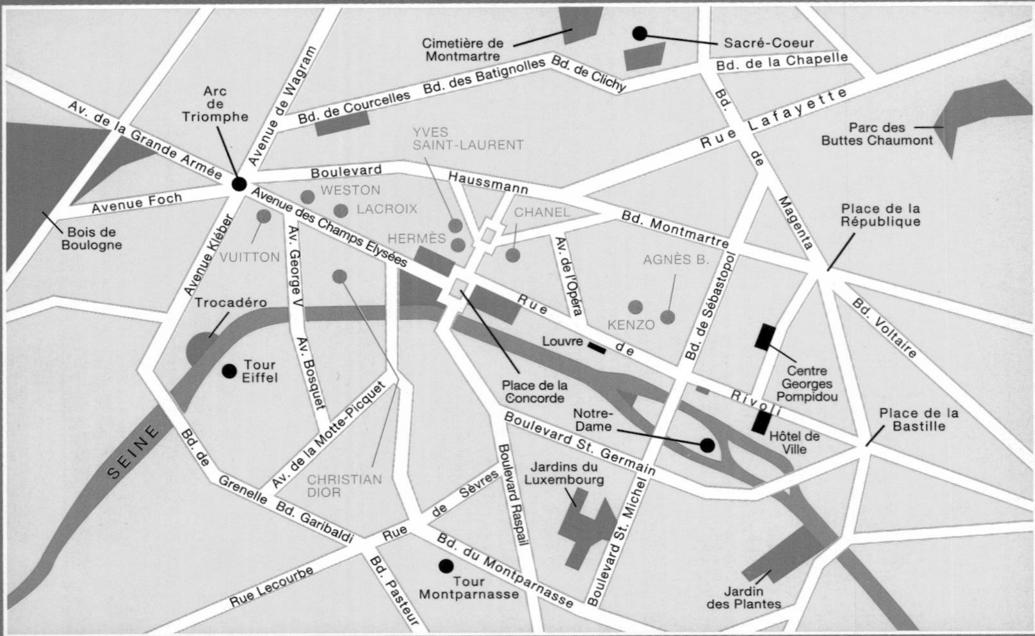
Cimetière de Montmartre
Sacré-Coeur
Bd. de la Chapelle
Bd. de Courcelles
Bd. des Batignolles
Bd. de Clichy
Arc de Triomphe
Avenue de Wagram
Av. de la Grande Armée
Rue Lafayette
Parc des Buttes Chaumont
YVES SAINT-LAURENT
Boulevard Haussmann
Bd. de Magenta
Avenue Foch
WESTON
LACROIX
CHANEL
Place de la République
Bois de Boulogne
Avenue des Champs Elysées
Bd. Montmartre
HERMÈS
VUITTON
Av. George V
Av. de l'Opéra
AGNÈS B.
Bd. de Sébastopol
Avenue Kléber
Trocadéro
Rue de Rivoli
KENZO
Bd. Voltaire
Louvre
Tour Eiffel
Av. Bosquet
Centre Georges Pompidou
Place de la Concorde
Notre-Dame
Place de la Bastille
Hôtel de Ville
Boulevard St. Germain
SEINE
Av. de la Motte-Picquet
Bd. de Grenelle
Jardins du Luxembourg
CHRISTIAN DIOR
Rue de Sèvres
Boulevard Raspail
Bd. Garibaldi
Boulevard St. Michel
Bd. du Montparnasse
Tour Montparnasse
Rue Lecourbe
Bd. Pasteur
Jardin des Plantes

**CHANEL** 31 rue Cambon, 1er.
■ 0930-1830 Mon.-Fri., 1000-1830 Sat. M Madeleine.
*World-famous as the birthplace of* haute couture, *it also sells ready-to-wear clothing in a magnificent setting.*

**YVES SAINT-LAURENT** 32 rue du Faubourg St. Honoré, 8e.
■ 1000-1900 Mon.-Sat. (closed Mon. am). M Madeleine.
*Beautiful clothes and shoes signed by one of France's top designers.*

**HERMÈS** 24 rue du Faubourg St. Honoré, 8e.
■ 1000-1830 Mon.-Sat. (closed Mon. am). M Madeleine.
*Exceptional quality, status-symbol scarves and leather goods.*

**LACROIX** 73 rue du Faubourg St. Honoré, 8e.
■ 1000-1900 Mon.-Fri., 1000-1300, 1400-1900 Sat. M Madeleine.
Haute couture *and off-the-peg garments by designer with southern style.*

**CHRISTIAN DIOR** 30 av. Montaigne, 8e.
■ 1030-1900 Mon.-Sat. (closed Mon. am). M Franklin D. Roosevelt.
*A major attraction: superb scarves, jewellery and accessories.*

**AGNÈS B.** 6 rue du Jour, 1er.
■ 1000-1900 Mon.-Sat. (closed Mon. am). M Les Halles.
*Leisurewear in a wide variety of styles and fashions.*

**VUITTON** 78 bis av. Marceau, 8e.
■ 0930-1830 Mon.-Sat. (closed Mon. am). M Etoile.
*The ultimate designer of bags, luggage and accessories.*

**WESTON** 114 av. des Champs Elysées, 8e.
■ 0930-1900 Tue.-Sat., 1000-1900 Mon. M George V.
*The most prestigious shoe shop in Paris.*

**KENZO** 3 pl. des Victoires, 2e.
■ 1000-1900 Tue.-Sat., 1100-1900 Mon. M Bourse.
*Fantastic flowing clothes. Japanese designer has seduced the Parisians!*

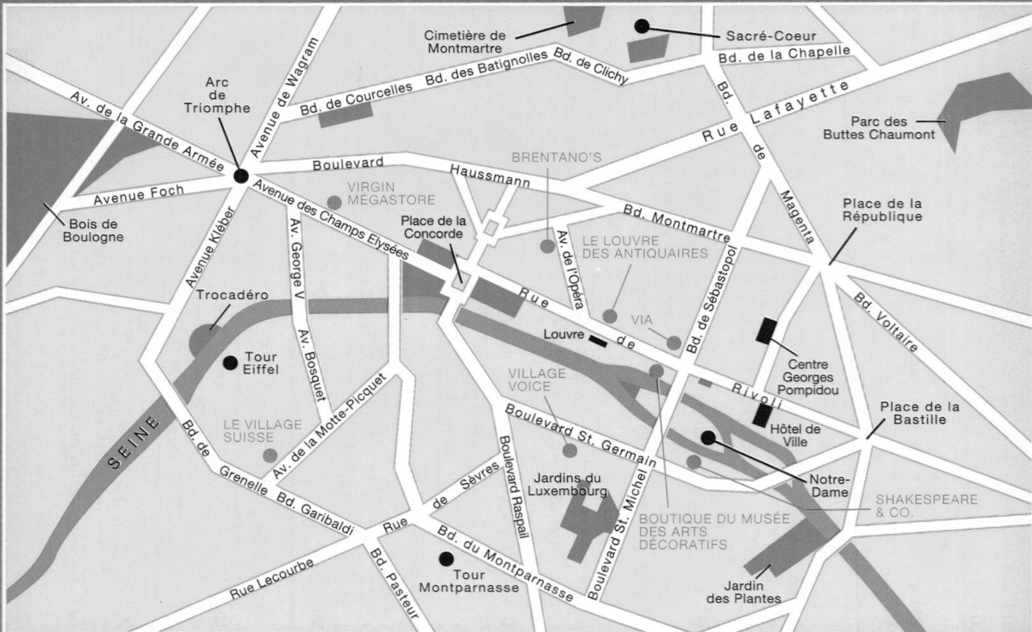
Cimetière de Montmartre
Sacré-Coeur
Bd. de la Chapelle
Bd. des Batignolles
Bd. de Clichy
Bd. de Courcelles
Arc de Triomphe
Avenue de Wagram
Av. de la Grande Armée
Rue Lafayette
Bd. de Magenta
Parc des Buttes Chaumont
Boulevard Haussmann
BRENTANO'S
Avenue Foch
VIRGIN MÉGASTORE
Bois de Boulogne
Avenue des Champs Elysées
Place de la Concorde
Bd. Montmartre
Place de la République
Avenue Kléber
Av. George V
Av. de l'Opéra
LE LOUVRE DES ANTIQUAIRES
Bd. de Sébastopol
Trocadéro
Rue de Rivoli
VIA
Louvre
Bd. Voltaire
Tour Eiffel
Av. Bosquet
Centre Georges Pompidou
VILLAGE VOICE
Av. de la Motte-Picquet
LE VILLAGE SUISSE
SEINE
Bd. de Grenelle
Boulevard St. Germain
Hôtel de Ville
Place de la Bastille
Notre-Dame
Jardins du Luxembourg
Rue de Sèvres
Boulevard Raspail
Bd. Garibaldi
SHAKESPEARE & CO.
Boulevard St. Michel
BOUTIQUE DU MUSÉE DES ARTS DÉCORATIFS
Bd. du Montparnasse
Rue Lecourbe
Bd. Pasteur
Tour Montparnasse
Jardin des Plantes

## Miscellaneous

**LE LOUVRE DES ANTIQUAIRES** 2 pl. du Palais Royal, 1er.
■ 1100-1900 Tue.-Sun. M Palais Royal.
*World-famous art market comprising 250 antique shops.*

**LE VILLAGE SUISSE** 78 av. de Suffren, 7e and 55 av. de La Motte-Picquet, 15e.
■ 1100-1900 Thu.-Mon. M La Motte-Picquet Grenelle.
*Originally built for the 1900 exhibition. Contains a selection of antique dealers.*

**VIA** 4-8 cour du Commerce St. André, 6e.
■ 0930-1900 Mon.-Sat. M Odéon. RER Châtelet-Les Halles.
*Avant-garde designs brought together from all over Europe.*

**BOUTIQUE DU MUSÉE DES ARTS DÉCORATIFS**
107 rue de Rivoli, 1er.
■ 1200-1800 Mon. & Wed.-Sat. M Palais Royal, Tuileries.
*Type of design centre: stationery, cutlery, industrial objects, materials.*

**VIRGIN MÉGASTORE** 56-60 av. des Champs Elysées, 8e.
■ 1000-2400 Mon.-Fri., 1200-2400 Sat. M Franklin D. Roosevelt.
*Records and books in an immense 30,000 sq. ft of selling space.*

**BRENTANO'S** 37 av. de l'Opéra, 2e.
■ 1000-1900 Mon.-Sat. M Opéra.
*Bilingual bookstore with an American atmosphere.*

**SHAKESPEARE & CO.** 37 rue de la Bûcherie, 5e.
■ 1200-2400. M Maubert-Mutualité.
*Friendly English-language bookshop containing a vast and varied selection of second-hand titles.*

**VILLAGE VOICE** 6 rue Princesse, 6e.
■ 1100-2000 Tue.-Sat., 1400-2000 Mon. M Mabillon.
*English-language bookshop named after (but not associated with) the famous American newspaper.*

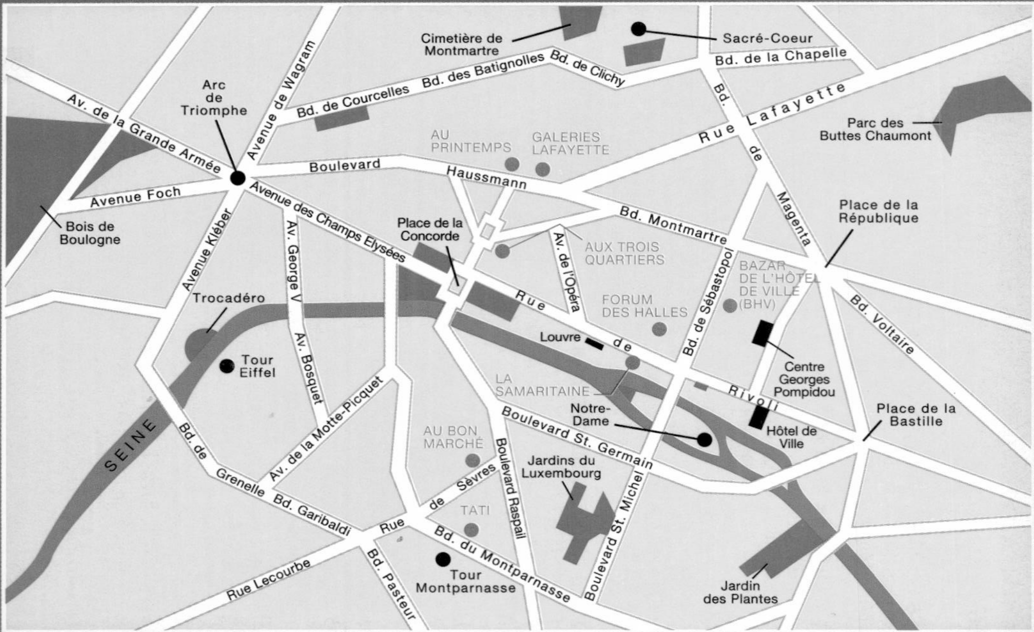

Cimetière de Montmartre
Sacré-Coeur
Bd. de la Chapelle
Bd. de Courcelles
Bd. des Batignolles
Bd. de Clichy
Arc de Triomphe
Avenue de Wagram
Av. de la Grande Armée
Rue Lafayette
Bd. de Magenta
Parc des Buttes Chaumont
AU PRINTEMPS
GALERIES LAFAYETTE
Boulevard Haussmann
Avenue Foch
Bois de Boulogne
Avenue des Champs Elysées
Place de la Concorde
Bd. Montmartre
Place de la République
Avenue Kléber
Av. George V
AUX TROIS QUARTIERS
Av. de l'Opéra
Bd. de Sébastopol
BAZAR DE L'HÔTEL DE VILLE (BHV)
Trocadéro
Rue de Rivoli
FORUM DES HALLES
Bd. Voltaire
Louvre
Tour Eiffel
Av. Bosquet
Centre Georges Pompidou
LA SAMARITAINE
Notre-Dame
Hôtel de Ville
Place de la Bastille
Av. de la Motte-Picquet
Boulevard St. Germain
SEINE
AU BON MARCHÉ
Jardins du Luxembourg
Bd. de Grenelle
Bd. Garibaldi
Rue de Sèvres
Boulevard Raspail
Boulevard St. Michel
TATI
Bd. du Montparnasse
Tour Montparnasse
Rue Lecourbe
Bd. Pasteur
Jardin des Plantes

## Department Stores

**AU PRINTEMPS** 64 bd. Haussmann, 9e.
■ 0935-1900 Mon.-Sat. M Chaussée d'Antin, Havre-Caumartin.
*Worth visiting for women's/men's fashions, accessories and perfumes.*

**GALERIES LAFAYETTE** 40 bd. Haussmann, 9e.
■ 0930-1845 Mon.-Sat. M Chaussée d'Antin, Havre-Caumartin.
*Paris' major department store, popular with tourists and locals. The huge hall with its glass roof was designed by Charnut in 1910-12.*

**LA SAMARITAINE** 19 rue de la Monnaie, 1er.
■ 0930-1900 Mon., Wed., Thu. & Sat., 0930-2030 Tue. & Fri.
M Pont Neuf.
*An amazing building housing a famous department store: most definitely a consumers' paradise.*

**AU BON MARCHÉ** 38 rue de Sèvres, 7e.
■ 0930-1830 Mon.-Sat. M Sèvres Babylone.
*Established in 1852, this is the oldest department store in Paris. Fascinating antique shop.*

**AUX TROIS QUARTIERS** 17 bd. de la Madeleine, 1er.
■ 0945-1830 Mon.-Sat. M Madeleine.
*Traditional French department store: interesting range of goods.*

**BAZAR DE L'HÔTEL DE VILLE (BHV)** 52-64 rue de Rivoli, 4e.
■ 0900-1900 Mon., Tue., Thu.-Sat., 0900-2200 Wed. M Hôtel de Ville.
*Wide range of furniture, household goods and DIY on five floors.*

**TATI** 140 rue de Rennes, 6e.
■ 0900-1900 Mon.-Sat. M Montparnasse Bienvenüe.
*Superb bargain clothes, well-stocked and cheap. Often crowded.*

**FORUM DES HALLES** 1-7 rue Pierre Lescot, 1er.
■ 1000-1930 Tue.-Sat., 1300-1930 Mon. RER Châtelet-Les Halles.
*Huge shopping complex on three levels containing no less than 180 shops, 15 restaurants and 10 cinemas.*

AVENUE
DES CHAMPS-ELYSEES

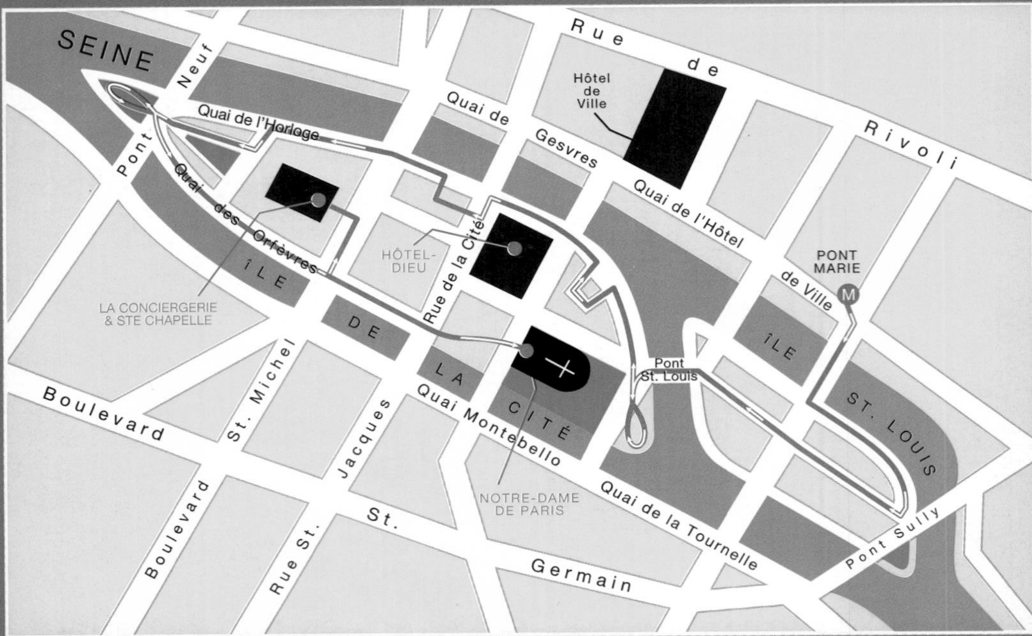
SEINE
Pont Neuf
Quai de l'Horloge
Quai des Orfèvres
ÎLE DE LA CITÉ
LA CONCIERGERIE & STE CHAPELLE
HÔTEL-DIEU
Rue de la Cité
Quai de Gesvres
Hôtel de Ville
Rue de Rivoli
Quai de l'Hôtel de Ville
PONT MARIE
ÎLE ST. LOUIS
Pont St. Louis
NOTRE-DAME DE PARIS
Quai Montebello
Quai de la Tournelle
Pont Sully
Boulevard St. Michel
Rue St. Jacques
Boulevard St. Germain

## *The Islands*

Duration: 2 hr. Begin at M Pont Marie.

Cross the bridge and turn left into quai d'Anjou before descending the steps to the quay, where you can enjoy a gentle stroll along the river.

Return to the road at Pont Sully and turn right into the long, narrow rue St. Louis-en-l'Île, the main street of Île St. Louis (see **A-Z**), lined with grand 17thC houses and interesting little shops. At No. 31 is Berthillon, with the best ice cream in Paris. Cross Pont St. Louis onto Île de la Cité (see **A-Z**), then left to the square de l'Île de France and the deeply moving Mémorial de la Déportation (built to commemorate the 200,000 French citizens who died in Nazi concentration camps).

After leaving the square, turn right into quai aux Fleurs, then left at rue des Chantres, right at rue Chanoinesse and right again into rue de la Colombe. These small and narrow streets still retain something of the atmosphere of old Paris. Turn left along quai de Corse, past the Hôtel-Dieu (hospice) and left again into pl. Louis Lépine. A flower market is held in this square six days a week with a bird market on Sun. (see **MARKETS**).

From here you can see the sombre façade of the prefecture of police and, if you continue along the quay to the Tour de l'Horloge, you will come to the first public clock in Paris (1334).

Carry on, taking a left turn into rue Harlay, then right at the lovely pl. Dauphine (home of the actress Simone Signoret until her death in 1985). At the far end of the *place* go through the passage, then cross the street and descend the stairs behind the statue of Henri IV. The stairway takes you into the square du Vert-Galant.

Returning to Pont Neuf, walk along quai des Orfèvres and turn left when you reach bd. du Palais. From here, you can visit La Conciergerie (see **A-Z**) and also the beautiful church of Ste Chapelle (see **A-Z**), before retracing your steps to Pont St. Michel.

Next, turn left along quai Marché Neuf, cross rue de la Cité and head towards pl. du Parvis Notre-Dame, from where there are superb views of the incomparable Notre-Dame cathedral. Note the brass star set within the cobbles at the front of the building. This is known as 'Point Zero', from where all the road distances in France are measured.

Round off your walk with a visit to the magnificent Notre-Dame de Paris (see **A-Z**) itself.

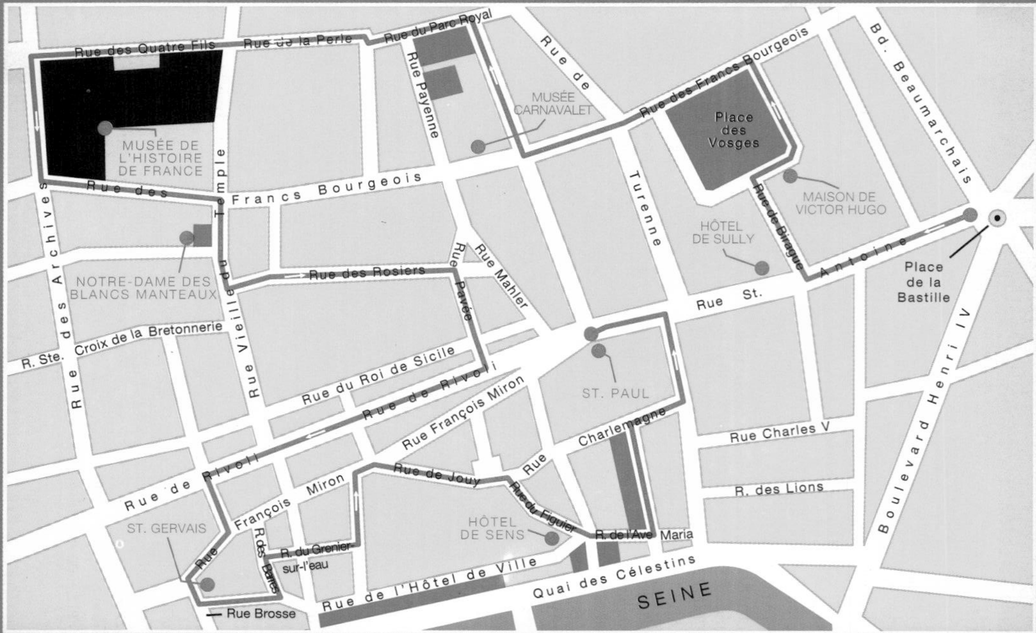

Rue des Quatre Fils
Rue de la Perle
Rue du Parc Royal
Rue Payenne
MUSÉE CARNAVALET
Rue de
Rue des Francs Bourgeois
Place des Vosges
Bd. Beaumarchais
MUSÉE DE L'HISTOIRE DE FRANCE
Rue des Francs Bourgeois
Rue Vieille du Temple
MAISON DE VICTOR HUGO
HÔTEL DE SULLY
Turenne
Rue de Birague
Rue St. Antoine
Place de la Bastille
NOTRE-DAME DES BLANCS MANTEAUX
Rue des Rosiers
Rue Pavée
Rue Mahler
Rue des Archives
R. Ste. Croix de la Bretonnerie
Rue du Roi de Sicile
Rue de Rivoli
Rue François Miron
ST. PAUL
Boulevard Henri IV
Rue Charlemagne
Rue Charles V
R. des Lions
Rue de Jouy
Rue du Figuier
R. de l'Ave Maria
HÔTEL DE SENS
ST. GERVAIS
Rue François Miron
R. des Barres
R. du Grenier-sur-l'eau
Rue de l'Hôtel de Ville
Quai des Célestins
SEINE
Rue Brosse

## Le Marais

Duration: 2 hr, excluding visits. Begin at M St. Paul.
Head down rue St. Antoine towards the Hôtel de Sully (which dates from the early 17thC) at No. 62. Turn right into rue de Birague and the imposing pl. des Vosges. To the right, under the arches, is the Maison de Victor Hugo (see MUSEUMS 2). Turn left through the narrow, bustling rue des Francs Bourgeois, then right at rue de Sévigné. No. 23 houses the Musée Carnavalet (see MUSEUMS 2). Turn left along rue du Parc Royal to pl. de Thorigny. Continue along rue de la Perle and rue des Quatre Fils, turning left at rue des Archives to the Musée de l'Histoire de France (1345-1745 Wed.-Sun.; 12F) in the Hôtel de Soubise. Continue along rue des Francs Bourgeois past the little church of Notre-Dame des Blancs Manteaux then turn right at rue Vieille du Temple, and left into rue des Rosiers. This is the heart of the Jewish quarter, with many interesting kosher delicatessens, bakers, etc. Turn right at rue Pavée, one of the first paved streets in the city. Bear right into rue de Rivoli and continue to pl. Baudoyer. At the far right side, walk to St. Gervais church (built 15th-17thC and where François Couperin was organist from 1689 to 1723) and then into rue Brosse. Turn left and left again into rue des Barres and then right into rue du Grenier sur l'Eau. Turn left again and then right into rue François Miron, where you can see at Nos 11 and 13 two of the oldest houses in Paris, dating from the 14thC. Turn down rue de Jouy, cross rue de Fourcy and turn right into rue du Figuier to the Hôtel de Sens, housing the Bibliothèque Forney (see **Libraries**). Turn left at rue de l'Ave Maria, pass rue des Jardins St. Paul and go left through the arch into the renovated courtyards of Village St. Paul. At the far end enjoy the lovely rue Charlemagne, before turning right then left at rue St. Paul, and left into rue St. Antoine, completing the walk at the 17thC church of St. Paul, near M St. Paul.

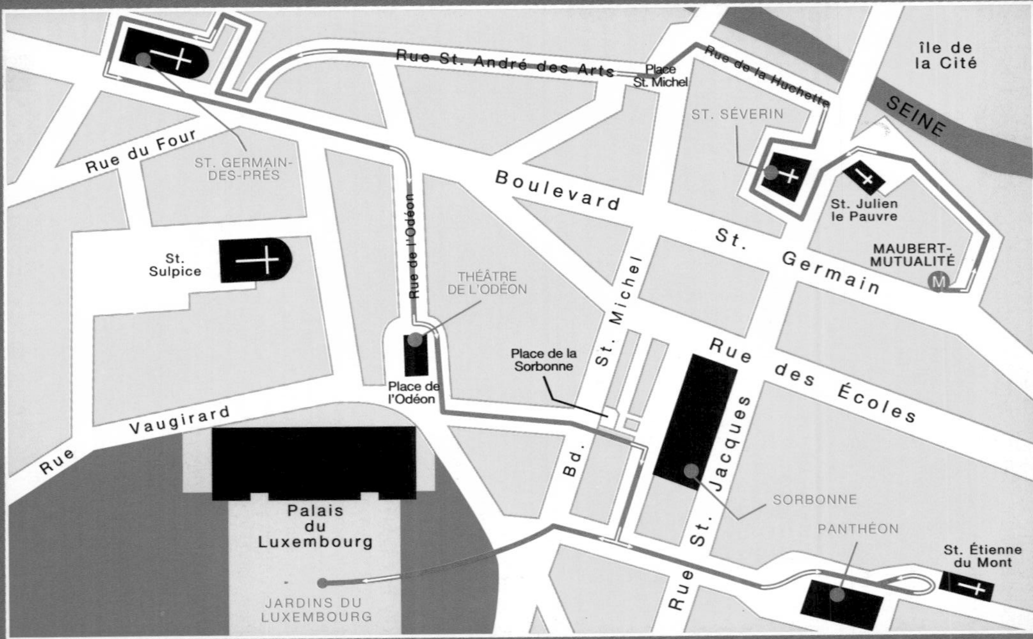
île de
la Cité
SEINE
Rue St. André des Arts
Place
St. Michel
Rue de la Huchette
ST. SÉVERIN
St. Julien
le Pauvre
MAUBERT-
MUTUALITÉ
M
Rue du Four
ST. GERMAIN-
DES-PRÉS
Boulevard St. Germain
St.
Sulpice
Rue de l'Odéon
THÉÂTRE
DE L'ODÉON
Place de
l'Odéon
Place de la
Sorbonne
Bd. St. Michel
Rue des Écoles
Rue St. Jacques
SORBONNE
PANTHÉON
St. Étienne
du Mont
Rue Vaugirard
Palais
du
Luxembourg
JARDINS DU
LUXEMBOURG

## Latin Quarter

Duration: 2 hr, excluding visits. Begin at M Maubert-Mutualité. From pl. Maubert, head along rue Frédéric Sauton towards the river, then left into rue de la Bûcherie. Cross rue Lagrange into the pleasant square Viviani. Turn left after the church into rue St. Jacques, right at rue de la Parcheminerie and right into rue Boutebrie. Turn right at rue St. Séverin, past the church of the same name (see **CHURCHES**), left at the narrow passageway, then left into rue de la Huchette with its numerous Greek kebab shops. At the end of the street is pl. St. Michel, centre of the Latin Quarter (see **A-Z**). Across the square is pl. St. André des Arts, where you'll find pavement cafés, restaurants, etc. Walk along rue St. André des Arts, then follow rue de Buci to bd. St. Germain, turning right then right again into passage de la Petite-Boucherie. The quaint, curving rue Cardinale leads left into the charming pl. de Fustembourg with its white globe lampposts and the Musée Delacroix. Turn right at rue de l'Abbaye into pl. St. Germain-des-Prés. The square contains much of interest, from the church of St. Germain-des-Prés (see **CHURCHES**) to the famous café Les Deux Magots (see **CAFÉS**). Go left along the boulevard to the carrefour de l'Odéon, then right at rue de l'Odéon towards the colonnaded portico of the Théâtre de l'Odéon. Turn left to rue de Vaugirard and across the bd. St. Michel to the lovely pl. de la Sorbonne, lined with cafés and full of students. From the square turn right along the front of the Sorbonne (see **A-Z**), then left at rue Soufflot where you have a superb view of the Panthéon (see **A-Z**). Go up the hill to the visitors' entrance on the far side. Returning down rue Soufflot, cross bd. St. Michel and complete your walk with a stroll round the beautiful Jardins du Luxembourg (see **A-Z**).

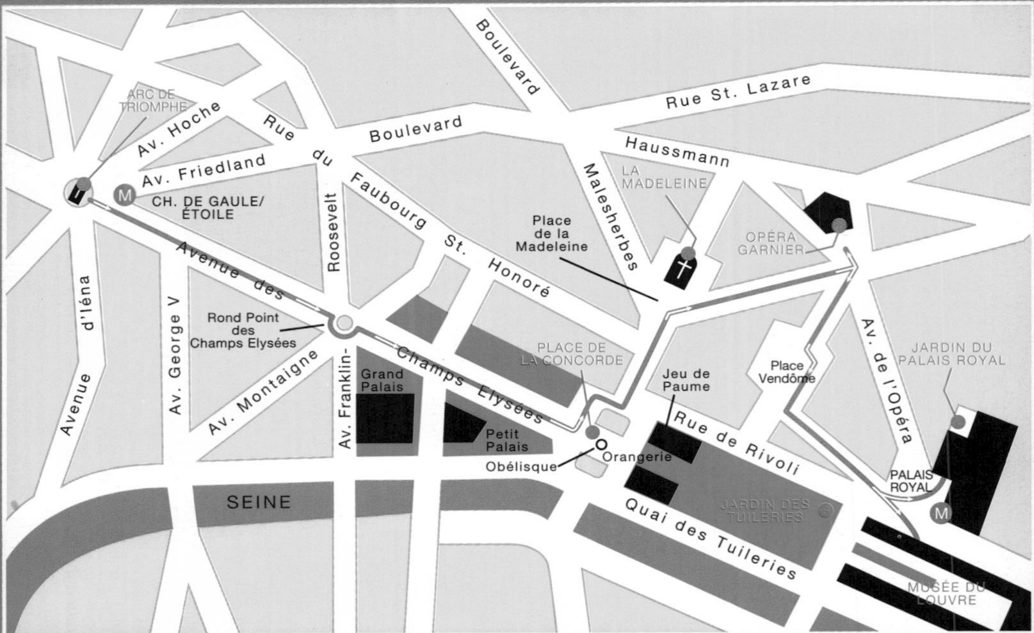
ARC DE TRIOMPHE
Av. Hoche
Rue du Faubourg St. Honoré
Boulevard
Boulevard Haussmann
Rue St. Lazare
Av. Friedland
CH. DE GAULE/ ÉTOILE
Roosevelt
Malesherbes
LA MADELEINE
Place de la Madeleine
OPÉRA GARNIER
Avenue des Champs Elysées
Avenue d'Iéna
Av. George V
Rond Point des Champs Elysées
Av. Montaigne
Av. Franklin-
Grand Palais
Petit Palais
PLACE DE LA CONCORDE
Jeu de Paume
Place Vendôme
Av. de l'Opéra
JARDIN DU PALAIS ROYAL
PALAIS ROYAL
Obélisque
Orangerie
Rue de Rivoli
JARDIN DES TUILERIES
Quai des Tuileries
SEINE
MUSÉE DU LOUVRE

# WALK 4

## *Av. des Champs Elysées*

Duration: 2 hr, excluding visits. Begin at M Charles de Gaulle-Etoile. Begin by climbing the 284 steps of the Arc de Triomphe (see **A-Z**) and sampling the magnificent views. Then head down av. des Champs Elysées (see **A-Z**), past the Tourist Office on the left, the famous Lido Cabaret on the right, and the café-restaurant, Le Fouquet's (see **CAFÉS**) at the junction of av. George V. Carry on to the Rond Point des Champs Elysées where the character of the avenue changes and it becomes more open and park-like. Stop to enjoy the view along av. Winston Churchill from pl. Clemenceau. On the other side of the *place* is the site of the Marché aux Timbres (see **MARKETS**). Continue to pl. de la Concorde (see **A-Z**) and admire the Marly horses, before looking west, back to the Arc de Triomphe; east to the Jardins des Tuileries (see **PARKS**) and Musée du Louvre (see **A-Z**); south to the columns of the Palais Bourbon; then north to the matching columns of La Madeleine where the American embassy occupies a prime location. Passing between the Hôtel Crillon and the Hôtel de la Marine, up rue Royale you will see the famous Maxim's restaurant and rue du Faubourg St. Honoré (see **Fashion**) on your left. Visit La Madeleine (see **CHURCHES**), completed in 1840 as a 'Temple of Glory' dedicated to Napoleon's army, before turning right along bd. de la Madeleine and bd. des Capucines to pl. de l'Opéra and the splendid façade of the Opéra Garnier (see **A-Z**). Taking a right turn down rue de la Paix, be sure to appreciate the windows full of luxury goods, then continue to pl. Vendôme (see **A-Z**) and the Ritz. At the far side of the square, exit right along rue St. Honoré, finishing at pl. du Palais Royal where you can either visit the Jardin du Palais Royal (see **PARKS**) or Musée du Louvre.

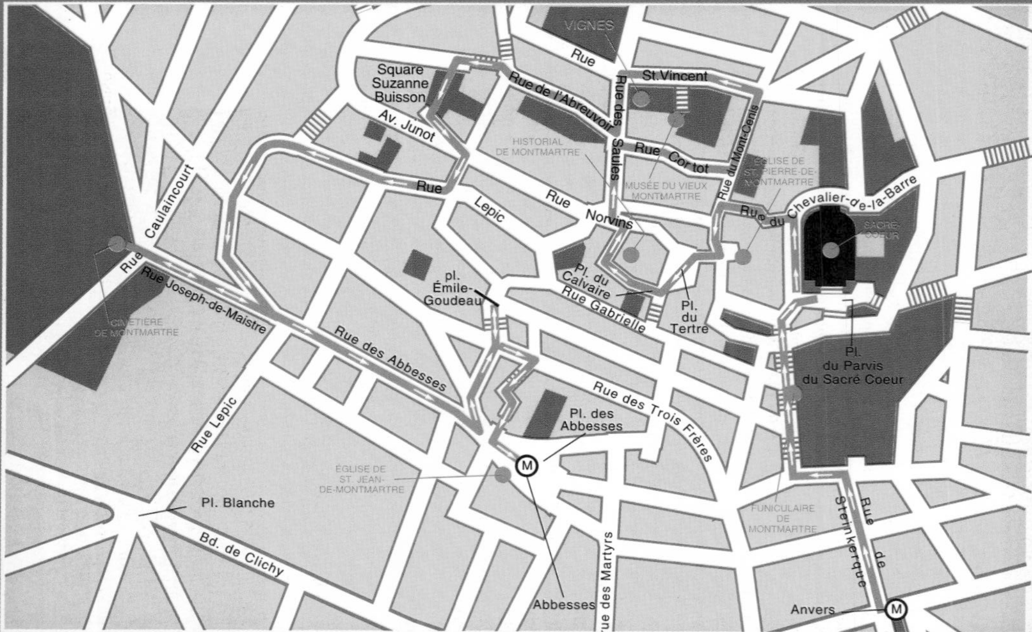

VIGNES
Rue St.Vincent
Square Suzanne Buisson
Rue de l'Abreuvoir
Rue des Saules
Av. Junot
HISTORIAL DE MONTMARTRE
Rue Cortot
MUSÉE DU VIEUX MONTMARTRE
Rue du Mont-Cenis
ÉGLISE DE ST-PIERRE-DE-MONTMARTRE
Rue du Chevalier-de-la-Barre
SACRÉ-COEUR
Rue Lepic
Rue Norvins
Rue Caulaincourt
Rue Joseph-de-Maistre
CIMETIÈRE DE MONTMARTRE
pl. Émile-Goudeau
Pl. du Calvaire
Rue Gabrielle
Pl. du Tertre
Pl. du Parvis du Sacré Coeur
Rue des Abbesses
Rue des Trois Frères
Pl. des Abbesses
M
ÉGLISE DE ST. JEAN-DE-MONTMARTRE
Rue Lepic
Pl. Blanche
Bd. de Clichy
Abbesses
Rue des Martyrs
FUNICULAIRE DE MONTMARTRE
Rue de Steinkerque
Anvers
M

## Montmartre

Duration: 1 hr 45 min. Begin at M Anvers.
Walk up rue de Steinkerque to the Funiculaire de Montmartre (funicular railway) and take a ride up the hill, or climb the steps via pl. du Parvis du Sacré-Coeur, to Sacré-Coeur (see **A-Z**), with its distinctive white domes. From here there is a superb view over the city, as well as the elegant interiors of the basilica to admire. A particular attraction is the enormous mosaic portraying Christ and His followers. Turn right into rue du Cardinal Guibert, then left at rue du Chevalier-de-la-Barre and left again at rue du Mont Cenis. From here admire the church of St. Pierre-de-Montmartre which had its origins in medieval times. Soak up the atmosphere of Montmartre (see **A-Z**) by strolling around pl. du Tertre, admiring the skills of the artists. Exit by rue du Calvaire and turn right into pl. du Calvaire, a quiet, country-like area with the Historial de Montmartre waxworks museum (1000-1900; 35F) at 11 rue Poulbot, where the exhibits reflect the history of the area. From here walk right along rue Poulbot, then down rue des Saules and right along rue Cortot to the Musée du Vieux Montmartre (1100-1800 Tue.-Sun.; 25F), which is worth a look. The museum is housed in the oldest building in the area, dating from the 18thC, and in the past has been the home to many artists, including Renoir, Utrillo, Suzanne Valadon and Dufy. At the end of rue Cortot turn left into rue du Mont Cenis and down the steps to rue St. Vincent. Go left through the Montmartre vineyard, which is the last one in Paris. A lively wine festival is held here every year at the beginning of Oct. (see **Events**). Rejoin rue des Saules and turn left uphill and right along rue de l'Abreuvoir to allée des Brouillards. At the far end, turn left into square Suzanne Buisson. On leaving the square at the opposite end, turn right into rue Girardon, cross av. Junot and turn right into rue Lepic at Moulin Radet (Van Gogh lived at No. 54). Continue along rue Lepic, which curves round to the left, then turn right into rue Joseph-de-Maistre. This street leads to rue Caulaincourt where you should turn left and walk down the steps at the end of the bridge to the Cimetière de Montmartre. Return along rue Joseph-de-Maistre and rue des Abbesses, then go left up rue Ravignan to pl. Émile Goudeau, right down passage des Abbesses to the lovely pl. des Abbesses and its church of St. Jean-de-Montmartre, and finish your walk at M Abbesses.

**Arc de Triomphe:** A magnificent triumphal arch, commissioned by Napoleon (see **A-Z**) in 1806 as a tribute to his army. Eventually completed in 1836 during the reign of Louis Philippe, it stands 50 m high and 45 m wide and is decorated with sculpted reliefs depicting military events. The Unknown Soldier lies under the arch and the Eternal Flame burns in front. From the top you can enjoy the views down the av. des Champs Elysées (see **A-Z**) to pl. de la Concorde (see **A-Z**) and the Musée du Louvre (see **A-Z**). Pl. Charles de Gaulle-Etoile, 8e. 1000-1700; 22F. M Etoile. See **WALK 4**.

**Arrondissements:** The area of Paris bounded by the ring road (*boulevard périphérique*) is divided into 20 administrative districts called arrondissements. Each one is very individual, with its own town hall and a distinct atmosphere. Starting at the Musée du Louvre (see **A-Z**) they radiate in a clockwise direction and are referred to as 1st, 2nd, 3rd, etc. In French these are 1er (*premier*), 2e (*deuxième*), 3e (*troisième*), etc., and are included in city addresses. See **CITY DISTRICTS**.

**Bastille, La:** Built in the 14thC, it was initially used as a fortress, then from the 17thC onwards a State prison housing political prisoners, many of whom were kept without trial. Inmates included Voltaire, the Marquis de Sade and the mysterious 'Man in the Iron Mask'. On 14 July 1789 a revolutionary mob stormed the prison, lynching the governor and freeing the seven prisoners. This event marked the start of the French Revolution, and its anniversary is celebrated each year on Bastille Day (see **Quatorze Juillet**).

**Bastille, place de la:** Place de la Bastille is a major traffic intersection standing on the site of the Bastille (see **A-Z**). Paving stones show where the building originally stood. The *place* is now dominated by the July Column, and is also the site of the city's new opera house, the Opéra Bastille (see **MUSIC VENUES**), which opened to the public on 14 July 1989, the bicentenary of the beginning of the French Revolution.

**Bateaux-Mouches:** These glass-roofed boats sail up and down the Seine (see **A-Z**) providing sightseeing tours. During the evening there are floodlit trips, and you can also dine on board.
Boats depart from Pont de l'Alma on the right bank (M Alma Marceau) every 30 min 1000-1200, 1400-1800 daily; duration 1 hr 15 min; 30F.
Floodlit trips depart every 30 min 2030-2200; duration 1 hr; 25F.
Meals: Lunch on board, dep. 1300 Tue.-Sun.; duration 1hr 45 min; cost 300F, inc. wine and service. Dinner (reservations and smart dress required), dep. 2030 Tue.-Sun.; duration 2hr 30 min; 500F, inc. wine and service, tel: 42259610.
Other companies offer similar trips: *Pariscope* (see **Newspapers**, **What's On**) has details under 'Promenades'. See **MUSTS**.

**Bibliothèque Nationale:** The national library, where every book published in France since 1537 is kept, today holds over 7,000,000 volumes. As well as books, the library houses the Medailles Collection (coins, medals, medallions and other works of art) and also the stateroom with the famous statue of the writer Voltaire, whose heart is buried within the pedestal. See **Libraries**.

**Bois de Boulogne:** 'Le Bois', as it is known locally, is situated to the west of the 16e arrondissement (see **A-Z**) and occupies 800 hectares of wooded parkland. As well as offering attractive walks and picnic spots, there are the Jardin d'Acclimatation (see CHILDREN), Musée National des Arts et Traditions Populaires (see MUSEUMS 2), Bagatelle gardens, a riding school, bicycle hire, boating on the ornamental lake, the race-courses of Auteuil and Longchamp (see **Sports**), and restaurants. It is not advisable to wander into the 'Bois' at night. M Porte Maillot, Porte d'Auteuil, Porte Dauphine.

**Bois de Vincennes:** This is the second major park in Paris, sitting on the right bank of the Seine (see **A-Z**), to the southeast of the city. Here you will find the Château de Vincennes, the floral gardens with roses and azaleas on display, a horticultural school, boating lakes, a racecourse, an arboretum, *boules* pitches, a Buddhist centre with Tibetan temple, the Cartoucherie de Vincennes (once an ammunition factory, now a theatre complex), and the Parc Zoologique de Paris (see CHILDREN). M Porte Dorée, Château de Vincennes.

**Champs Elysées, av. des:** This 2 km-long avenue stretches between pl. de la Concorde (see **A-Z**) and the Etoile (see **A-Z**), and was once regarded as the most beautiful in the world. Dating from the 17thC, it was planted with trees to extend the view from the Jardin des Tuileries (see PARKS). In 1709 the area was named the Champs Elysées (Elysian Fields) and by 1828 the avenue had gas-lighting, pavements and aristocratic residences, making it a very fashionable promenade. Today the area is somewhat commercialized, and the section between Rond Point and Etoile is lined with shops, banks, cinemas, fast-food outlets, car showrooms and airline offices. Even so, the views from Etoile or pl. de la Concorde are quite magnificent and the pavement cafés provide a most interesting spot from which to sit and watch the world go by. 8e. M/RER Charles de Gaulle-Etoile, George V, Franklin D. Roosevelt, Clemenceau, Concorde. See MUSTS, WALK 4.

**Chantilly:** The famous chateau on the lakeside here is in two parts: the Grand Château and the Petit Château d'Enghien. You can also visit

the Musée Condé, which has an interesting collection of 15th-17thC paintings, sculptures, drawings, ceramics and furniture, and the Cabinet de Livres, which houses over 12,500 rare books and manuscripts. Among them is the Duc de Berri's *Book of Hours* – one of the finest illuminated manuscripts in the world. See **EXCURSIONS 1**.

**Chartres:** The town of Chartres is best known for its Gothic cathedral, one of the world's finest. It has magnificent stained-glass windows dating from the 12th and 13thC, and beautifully carved portals, nave and choir. See **EXCURSION 4**.

**Compiègne:** This extremely large 18thC palace was initially built during the reign of Louis XV and later restored by Napoleon (see **A-Z**). Louis XVI entertained Marie-Antoinette here, and likewise Napoleon his second wife, Empress Marie-Louise. There are ten apartments restored to their former glory and many of the tapestries and pieces of furniture were brought by Napoleon himself. The palace also houses the Musée National de la Voiture et du Tourisme (Transport Museum) where you can see coaches, carriages, early bicycles and automobiles. 82 km northeast of Paris. SNCF: From Gare du Nord to Compiègne. Car: A 11. 0930-1630 Wed.-Mon.; 25F.

**Conciergerie, La:** One of the most famous prisons in France and part of the old royal palace. Many leading figures of the Revolution, including Marie-Antoinette and Robespierre, were kept here before being led to the guillotine. Today you can visit the huge, vaulted Gothic room of the Salles des Gens d'Armes, the Salles des Gardes, and the kitchen with its enormous fireplace, all dating from the 14thC. 1 quai de l'Horloge, 1er. M Cité. 0900-1800 (1700 winter); 23F. See **WALK 1**.

**Concorde, place de la:** An impressive square with views to La Madeleine (see **CHURCHES**), Palais Bourbon, Musée du Louvre (see **A-Z**) and Arc de Triomphe (see **A-Z**). When laid out in 1755-75 it displayed a statue of Louis XV, then one of La Liberté (during the Revolution), and today it boasts the Obelisk of Luxor. The Marly horses were sculpted by Guillaume Ier Cousteau (1667-1746) who mainly produced work for Versaille (see **A-Z**) and Marly-le-Roi (see **EXCURSIONS 2**), where the horses originally came from – hence their name. Louis XVI, Marie-Antoinette, Robespierre and Danton were all victims of the guillotine which once stood here. 8e. M Concorde.

**De Gaulle, Charles (1890-1970):** Soldier and statesman. As leader of the Free French with his headquarters in England during World War II, he was the symbol of resistance to German occupation and the Vichy regime. After the Liberation in 1944, he formed a provisional government, but soon retired from politics, critical of France's weak parliamentary system. In 1958, with France on the verge of civil war over Algerian demands for independence, he became the first president of the Fifth Republic. Unable to contain the student revolt of 1968, he resigned after losing a referendum in 1969.

**Dôme des Invalides:** Also known as Église du Dôme. A domed church, built 1675-1706, which houses the tomb of Napoleon (see **A-Z**), a sarcophagus of red porphyry upon a green Vosges granite pedestal. The dome has a leaded roof and is decorated with gilded trophies and garlands. See **CHURCHES**.

**Eiffel, Tour:** Internationally recognized as the symbol of France, the tower was designed by Gustave Eiffel to mark the centenary of the French Revolution. Opened in May 1889, standing 312 m high, it was the tallest building of its day. There are three platforms, all offering exceptional views, those from the top being positively breathtaking. On a clear day you can see landmarks well outside the suburbs of the city. Champ-de-Mars, 7e. M Trocadéro, Bir Hakeim. 0900-2300 (3rd level closed mid Nov.-mid Mar.). Lift to 3rd level, 49F; 2nd level, 28F; 1st level, 18F. By stairs to 1st and 2nd levels, 8F. See **MUSTS**.

**Etoile:** Officially pl. Charles de Gaulle, this junction is known as l'Etoile (star) because of the 12 avenues which radiate from it. There are superb views from the top of the Arc de Triomphe (see **A-Z**) at its centre. 8e/16e/17e. M/RER Charles de Gaulle-Etoile. See **WALK 4**.

**Euro Disneyland:** Perhaps the most exciting tourism development of recent years, Euro Disneyland, opened on 12 April 1992 at Marne-la-Vallée, 32 km east of Paris, is set to to bring a unique leisure concept to Europe – the complete resort destination. Based on the extremely successful original Magic Kingdom, established at Disneyland in

California in 1955, the Euro Disneyland Theme Park is contained within the Euro Disney Resort, with its hotels and leisure amenities. Phase 1 of the resort encompasses an initial 600 hectares, with future developments giving an increased area of 2000 hectares, one-fifth the size of Paris, by 2017. Thirty kilometres of roads and a railroad round its perimeter transport the estimated 11 million annual visitors, while no less than 12,000 employees, or 'cast members', doing everything from steering the Mark Twain sternwheeler to selling popcorn, ensure that nobody leaves unhappy.

The theme park has 30 attractions divided between five 'themed' lands:

*Main Street USA:* A typical turn-of-the-century American town, complete with horsedrawn streetcars and displays of classic cars, serves as the entrance to the other 'lands'.

*Frontierland:* Inspired by Monument Valley, this area features the hair-raising runaway mine train, the rather more sedate paddlewheel-steamboats, and Phantom Manor, complete with haunted chambers.

*Adventureland:* Pirates of the Caribbean realistically depicts a raid on an 18thC Spanish port as you sail by unnoticed. You can also explore the Swiss Family Robinson's treehouse and Adventure Isle, or browse in the Adventureland Bazaar, inspired by *The Arabian Nights*.

*Fantasyland:* At the heart of this area is the 43 m-tall symbol of Euro Disneyland – Sleeping Beauty's Castle – designed like a French chateau and complete with lurking dragon! All the nearby attractions are based on Disney's interpretations of legends and fables, such as Snow White and the Seven Dwarfs and Pinocchio, and you'll also find It's a Small World, Walt Disney's 'salute' to children.

*Discoveryland:* Drawing on the works of Leonardo da Vinci, Jules Verne, H. G. Wells and contemporary science-fiction writers, this 'land' features Star Tours, an intergalactic voyage using flight simulator techniques and film special effects; Videopolis, devoted to the video image and turning into a disco for 2000 people at night; Le Visionarium, showing a 360°-screen film on Europe; and a 3D Michael Jackson film in the Cinemagique theatre.

Other on-site attractions include Le Festival Disney, an 18,000 sq. m futuristic complex with shops restaurants and entertainment, which is illuminated at night; an 18-hole championship golf course (to be

upgraded to 27 holes in 1993); and the man-made Lake Buena Vista. Accommodation (a total of 5200 rooms) at the Euro Disney Resort depicts various American themes and ranges from the turn-of-the-century style of the luxury Disneyland Hotel to Camp Davy Crockett, set in woods with nature trails and providing almost 200 pitches for tents and caravans, as well as over 400 trailers to rent. Between these poles are the 'skyscraper' Hotel New York, the Newport Bay Club, the Sequoia Lodge, Western-style Hotel Cheyenne and desert-themed Hotel Santa Fe. Prices range from 550F to 1950F per night for a four-person room, while four-six person cabins at Camp Davy Crockett range from 575F to 875F. Daily rates for admission to Euro Disneyland are 250F for everyone over ten, 170F for 3-9s and under-3s are free. *Reservations:* In writing to Euro Disney SCA, Central Reservations Office, BP105, 94350 Villiers-sur-Marne, France. By telephone on 49414910 (UK citizens) or 49414915 (Irish citizens). Different numbers are available for all European nationalities.
*Access:* Train; RER from Paris. A TGV high-speed railway line will open in 1994. Car; Take the A 4 signed Nancy-Metz, then the D 231, following the Euro Disney signs.

**Fashion:** Paris, fashion centre of the world, has many *haute couture* boutiques. They are mainly concentrated in rue du Faubourg St. Honoré (e.g. Hermès, Yves Saint-Laurent, Lanvin), av. Montaigne (Nina Ricci, Christian Dior), St. Germain-des-Prés, pl. des Victoires (Cacharel, Kenzo) and increasingly on the Left Bank (see **A-Z**). Many shops sell last year's designer clothes at vastly reduced prices (20-50% off) and you will find these around the 6e arrondissement (see **A-Z**) in the rues de Rennes, de Sèvres and St. Placide. See **SHOPPING 1-3, WALK 4**.

**Food:** No nation takes more pride in its cuisine than France, and Paris is undoubtedly one of the world's major gastronomic centres. *Haute cuisine* (classic, rich and extravagant) may be beyond the average tourist's pocket and *nouvelle cuisine* (fresh, lightly-cooked and imaginatively-presented) might well be regarded with suspicion, but the high standard of cooking in even the humblest of bistros is sure to please the visitor.

The archetypal breakfast consists of coffee and croissants. *Fromages* (cheeses), cold meats, patisseries (pastries) and baguette sandwiches will provide sustenance during the day. At dinner every kind of meat, game, poultry, offal, fish and shellfish is carefully prepared in a huge variety of guises. Some of the favourites are: *escargots* (snails); bisque (shellfish soup); *pâté de foie gras* (goose liver pâté); *moules marinière* (mussels and shallots in white wine); *coq au vin* (chicken in red wine); bouillabaisse (fish and vegetable stew); boeuf bourguignon (beef and vegetables in red wine); *canard à l'orange* (duck in orange sauce); *cassoulet* (pork, goose, sausage and haricot bean casserole); *tournedos Rossini* (fillet of beef stuffed with pâté); *blanquette de veaux* (veal in white sauce); crêpe suzette (flambéed pancake); and petits fours (sweetmeats). See **RESTAURANTS 1-4**, **Eating Out**.

**Île de la Cité:** A small island in the Seine (see **A-Z**) in the city centre which was possibly the first part of Paris to be inhabited, maybe earlier than the 3rdC BC. 1er/4e. M Cité. See **WALK 1**.

**Île St. Louis:** The second island in the Seine (see **A-Z**), joined to the Île de la Cité (see **A-Z**) as recently as the 17thC. There are still many old houses to see, with views over the Left Bank (see **A-Z**) and Notre-Dame de Paris (see **A-Z**), and its tranquillity makes it an ideal place for a peaceful stroll. 4e. M Pont Marie. See **WALK 1**.

**Invalides, Hôtel des:** Home of three military museums: Musée de l'Armée; Musée de l'Ordre de la Libération (covering various facets of World War II); and Musée des Plans Reliefs (maps, models and detailed plans of French fortifications and military strongholds). See **CHURCHES**, **MUSEUMS 2**.

**Jewish Quarter:** The Jewish Quarter, chiefly concentrated around the rue des Rosiers in the fourth arrondissement (see **A-Z**), with many kosher shops and restaurants. M St. Paul. See **WALK 2**.

**Latin Quarter:** Student centre on the Left Bank (see **A-Z**), opposite Île de la Cité (see **A-Z**), where many of the University of Paris buildings are situated. The students and professors spoke Latin in its early days, hence the name, and you'll find a wide range of cheap restaurants and hotels here. See **CITY DISTRICTS**, **WALK 3**.

**Left Bank:** The area immediately south of the Seine (see **A-Z**) which includes the Latin Quarter (see **A-Z**), St. Germain-des-Prés (see **A-Z**), Montagne Ste Geneviève and Montparnasse (see **A-Z**). The University of Paris is largely situated here and the area has long been associated with students, intellectuals, artists, etc., with a very different atmosphere to that of the commercial Right Bank (see **A-Z**). See **CITY DISTRICTS**, **MUSTS**, **WALK 3**.

**Libraries:** *Bibliothèque Nationale:* Certain areas of the library are open to the public, but a reader's card is required to use the books. 0900-2000 Mon.-Fri., 0900-1730 Sat. 58 rue de Richelieu, 2e. M Bourse, Palais Royal. See **A-Z**.
*BPI (Bibliothèque Publique d'Information):* A huge library with an extensive English-language section. 1200-2200 Mon., Wed.-Fri., 1000-2200 Sat. & Sun. Centre Georges Pompidou, pl. Beaubourg, 4e. M Rambuteau.
*Bibliothèque Mazarine:* A collection of rare books covering French regional history which is housed in a 17thC mansion. 1000-1800 Mon.-Fri. 23 quai Conti, 6e. M Pont Neuf.
*Bibliothèque Forney (Hôtel de Sens):* Books on fine arts and crafts kept in a medieval bishop's palace. 1330-2015 Tue.-Fri., 1000-2015 Sat. 1 rue du Figuier, 4e. M St. Paul. See **WALK 2**.
There are also libraries at the following cultural institutes: British, 9 rue de Constantine, 7e, and American, 10 rue du Général Camou, 7e. Both offer free access to an extensive selection of books and periodicals relating to Britain and America.

**Louvre, Musée du:** Built between the 16th and 19thC, this is undoubtedly one of the most famous art galleries in the world. The Palais du Louvre began as a royal residence, and after the Revolution opened as a national art gallery and museum in 1793. Today it is undergoing major expansion and reorganization, which includes the resiting of the entrance under the controversial glass pyramid east of pl. du Carrousell, designed by the Sino-American architect, Pei. The vast collection is in seven sections: three of antiquities (Oriental, Egyptian, Greek and Roman), sculpture, applied art, graphic art and paintings. The two undoubted 'stars' are the *Mona Lisa* (see **A-Z**) and the Venus de Milo, but there is so much to see that a number of trips is recommended. Be warned – it is usually crowded! See **ART GALLERIES, MUSTS.**

**Luxembourg, Jardins du:** Next to the Palais du Luxembourg, these lovely gardens have much to offer, including tennis courts, pony rides, puppet theatres, ponds and fountains. See **MUSTS, PARKS, WALK 3.**

**Malmaison, Château de:** The Empress Josephine, wife of Napoleon (see **A-Z**), lived here from 1799 until her death in 1814. You can visit both the private and official apartments on the guided tours, seeing many original furnishings in the dining, music and billiard rooms. Napoleon's grey raincoat and his black cocked hat are among the exhibits on view in the nearby Musée de Bois-Préau. RER to La Défense, then Bus 158A to Malmaison-Château. 1000-1200, 1330-1700 Wed.-Mon.; chateau 25F.

**Mona Lisa**: Leonardo da Vinci painted *La Joconde* (as it is known in France) in 1505 and it is probably the best-known painting in the world. It is permanently on view in the Salle des Etats on the first floor of the Musée du Louvre (see **A-Z**).

**Montmartre:** A picturesque area which still manages to retain a village-like atmosphere. It is dominated by the white-domed Sacré-Coeur (see **A-Z**). In the 19thC many writers, composers and artists frequented Montmartre, e.g. Baudelaire, Berlioz, Toulouse-Lautrec, Van

Gogh, Picasso and Modigliani, but nowadays tourists completely dominate the area. If you climb or take the funicular railway to the top of the hill (*butte*), you can enjoy some of the most breathtaking views over Paris. 18e. M Abbesses, Anvers. See **CITY DISTRICTS**, **MUSTS**, **WALK 5**.

**Montparnasse:** An area on the Left Bank (see **A-Z**) which replaced Montmartre (see **A-Z**) as the Bohemian centre of Paris in the late 19th and early 20thC. Some of the famous people who frequented the area include James Joyce, Hilaire Belloc, F. Scott Fitzgerald, Henry Miller and Ernest Hemingway, the latter of which lived at 113 rue Notre-Dame des Champs and wrote at La Closerie des Lilas (see **RESTAURANTS 4**). Until recently Europe's tallest building – Canary Wharf in London now holds the record – the 59-storey Tour Maine-Montparnasse dominates the area and has a shopping complex at its base, and a bar and shop on the 56th floor (0930-2330 April-Sep., 1000-2200 Oct.-Mar.; 31F to 59th floor, 50F to 56th). At the Cimetière du Montparnasse you can find the graves of Guy de Maupassant, Jean-Paul Sartre, Baudelaire and André Citroën, among others. 6e/14e/15e. M Montparnasse Bienvenüe, Raspail. See **CITY DISTRICTS**.

**Mouffetard, rue:** A narrow and lively street which winds downhill from pl. de la Contrescarpe, with little old shops, houses and small restaurants on either side. Try to visit the daily food market (see MARKETS) if you get a chance. 5e. M Censier Daubenton, Monge.

**Moulin Rouge:** Birthplace of the cancan, this famous nightclub was opened in 1883 and its early days were recorded in the paintings of Toulouse-Lautrec. Today it is still very popular, though mostly with tourists. 82 bd. de Clichy, 18e. M Blanche.

**Music:** Paris has music to satisfy all tastes:
*Classical:* At the Opéra Garnier (see **A-Z**) and the numerous concert halls (e.g. salles Pleyel and Cortot, Théâtre des Champs Elysées, Châtelet, Maison de la Radio). A comprehensive list can be found in *Pariscope* and *l'Officiel des Spectacles* (see **Newspapers**, **What's On**).
*Contemporary music:* IRCAM at the Centre Georges Pompidou is the place to go, while venues where more varied and popular styles can be heard include the Olympia, Théâtre de la Ville, Palais des Congrès and Zénith. Tickets are available from box offices and FNAC bookstores (Forum des Halles, av. Wagram, Maine-Montparnasse shopping centre). See MUSIC VENUES.

**Napoleon (1769-1821):** Probably France's most famous ruler. He was the son of a Corsican nobleman who rose through the ranks of the Revolutionary Army to become a brigadier at the age of 24. In 1799 he seized power in a coup d'état and crowned himself the first Emperor of France (1804). His attempt to conquer the whole of Europe was finally crushed at the Battle of Waterloo in 1815 and he died six years later in exile on the island of St. Helena. His remains were returned to France in 1840 and now lie in the tomb in the Dôme des Invalides (see **A-Z**).

**Notre-Dame de Paris:** Built between 1163 and 1345, this well-known Gothic cathedral has been at the centre of many important events: the conversion to Catholicism and coronation of Henri IV in 1594; the crowning of Napoleon (see **A-Z**) as first Emperor of France in 1804; and the Magnificat with Pope John Paul II in 1980.

After the Revolution (1789-99) the cathedral fell into neglect but was to witness a revival with the Romantic movement and interest generated through Victor Hugo's novel *The Hunchback of Notre-Dame*, resulting in public pressure for restoration from 1841 onwards.
The western façade is the most impressive with three carved portals depicting the Virgin Mary, the Last Judgment and St. Anne. Above is the Gallery of Kings and the superb rose window. The best view of the interior is from below the organ, where you can see the light flooding in through the stained glass. Try to climb to the top of the north tower where you not only have a marvellous view but come face-to-face with the grotesque carved gargoyles. See **CHURCHES, MUSTS, WALK 1**.

**Opéra Garnier, L':** The largest opera house in the world, built by Garnier for Napoleon III and completed in 1875. Both the exterior and interior are extremely grand and ornate, and during the day there are guided tours (1100-1630) of the inside of the building, including the underground grotto which is supposed to have inspired the story of *The Phantom of the Opera*. It is difficult to obtain tickets for performances; you will have to book at least two weeks in advance and be prepared to pay as much as 300F-600F each. See **MUSIC VENUES, WALK 4**.

**Orsay, Musée d':** The Hôtel and Gare d'Orsay (opened in 1900) is a huge building overlooking the Seine (see **A-Z**). After closing as a railway station in 1973 it was converted into a museum dedicated to all forms of 19thC artistic expression. The exhibits were brought from various locations, including the Musée du Louvre, Musée du Jeu de Paume, Palais de Tokyo and numerous regional museums, as well as private collections. Beneath the large glass roof is a veritable feast for the eyes, especially the extraordinary collection of Impressionists (Cézanne, Degas, Sisley, Monet, Renoir), sculptures by Rodin and Camille Claudel, and several Van Goghs. Some post-1900 paintings (Matisse, Klimt) and exhibits on the birth of cinema are also of great interest. See **ART GALLERIES**.

**Panthéon:** Dedicated to Ste Geneviève and built by Louis XV, this mausoleum for heroes of the French Republic is the last resting place of

Victor Hugo, Emile Zola, Rousseau, Voltaire, Louis Braille and Resistance leader Jean Moulin. Pl. du Panthéon, 5e. RER/M Luxembourg, Cardinal Lemoine. See WALK 3.

**Pigalle:** This is an extremely sleazy red-light district below Montmartre (see **A-Z**), with sex shops, porn cinemas and prostitutes. Stretching west from pl. Pigalle is the busy bd. de Clichy with restaurants and the famous Théâtre des Deux Ânes at No. 100. The notorious Moulin Rouge (see **A-Z**) is located in pl. Blanche. M Pigalle, Blanche, Pl. de Clichy. See NIGHTLIFE.

**Pompidou, Centre Georges:** Its full title is Centre National d'Art et de Culture Georges-Pompidou. This massive, ultra-modern building by controversial architects Richard Rogers (UK) and Renzo Piano (Italy) was opened in 1977 to house a 'multicultural centre'. It consists of five storeys of glass and steel with structural members, ventilation shafts and escalators prominent on the outside, and is brightly painted in red, yellow, green and blue. Inside are the Musée National d'Art Moderne (see ART GALLERIES), a library (see **A-Z**), a range of exhibition halls, an art bookshop and two institutes dedicated to various strands of research. Plateau Beaubourg, 4e. 1200-2200 Mon., Wed., Thu. & Fri., 1000-2200 Sat. & Sun.; free, except for the museum and some exhibitions. M Rambuteau.

**Pompidou, Georges (1911-74):** French statesman who succeeded de Gaulle (see **A-Z**) as president in 1969. He reversed de Gaulle's policy of resistance to British membership of the Common Market and was instrumental in securing acceptance of Britain's entry to the Community in 1973 after years of negotiation.

**Quatorze Juillet, Fête Nationale de:** 14 July, Bastille Day, is France's national holiday and commemorates the storming of the Bastille (see **A-Z**). Everything closes for the day and the whole country joins in the celebrations, which include firework displays, parties and military processions along the av. des Champs Elysées (see **A-Z**). See **Events**.

**Right Bank:** This is the commercial district which lies to the north of the Seine (see **A-Z**), and is where most of the offices are to be found. It is situated between the Jardin des Tuileries (see **PARKS**) and Opéra Garnier (see **A-Z**), and extends from Etoile (see **A-Z**) to Beaubourg (see **CITY DISTRICTS**).

**Rivoli, rue de:** A well-known shopping street, now overrun with souvenir shops. There are also tearooms, grand hotels and W. H. Smith (newsagent and bookshop). The arcade section, running from pl. de la Concorde (see **A-Z**) to the Musée du Louvre (see **A-Z**), was built to celebrate Napoleon's (see **A-Z**) victories in Italy. 1er. M Concorde, Tuileries, Palais Royal. See **SHOPPING 2 & 3**.

**Sacré-Coeur:** This magnificent white basilica was built by public subscription in 1876-91 as an act of contrition and expression of hope following France's disasters in the Franco-Prussian War of 1870-71. It was consecrated in 1919 and stands in a prominent position on top of the Butte de Montmartre, making it a familiar landmark. See **CHURCHES, WALK 5, Montmartre**.

**St. Denis Basilique:** Situated in the northern suburb of St. Denis, this 12thC cathedral marked the birth of Gothic architecture in Europe, and the first-ever rose window, in its western front, was to become a standard feature of Gothic churches. The cathedral has been the traditional setting for the crowning of French kings and the tombs of all but three are contained here. See **EXCURSIONS 1**.

**Ste Chapelle:** Originally built in 1243-48 as a shrine for holy relics and restored in the 19thC. It is best known for its stained-glass scenes from the Old and New testaments, and the 15thC rose window which portrays scenes from the Apocalypse. See **CHURCHES, WALK 1**.

**St. Germain-des-Prés:** Dating from the 6thC, this is the oldest church in Paris and was initially a Benedictine abbey before being rebuilt during the 11th, 12th and 17thC. It was extensively restored in 1822 after an explosion and fire, and today hosts a mixture of Romanesque, Gothic and 19thC decoration. See **CHURCHES, WALK 3**.

**St. Germain-en-Laye:** The chateau is now the home of the excellent Musée des Antiquités Nationales with its impressive collection of objects and artefacts from the Stone Age to Roman and Merovingian times. In the Stone Age section is a model of the famous

Lascaux Caves where the earliest examples of cave paintings were found. See **EXCURSIONS 2**.

**St. Sulpice:** A 17th-18thC church with an imposing western front and splendid organ, one of the world's largest. Look out for the meridian line engraved between the transepts. It is lit by the sun's rays at noon on different points depending on the time of year. See **CHURCHES**.

**Seine:** The river which starts near Dijon to the south of Paris and flows for 771 km to the sea at Le Havre. An 11 km stretch flows through Paris with its famous waterfront, the quais de Paris. Today the right bank has been taken over by a cross-city motorway but the left bank has been left relatively unspoilt and you can still enjoy romantic strolls on its cobbled quays.

**Sorbonne, La:** Founded in 1253 by Robert de Sorbon, this one-time theological college is now one of the world's greatest universities. Student unrest here in 1968 led to university reform in France.
17 rue de la Sorbonne, 5e. M Odéon, RER Luxembourg. See **WALK 3**.

**Vendôme, place:** A magnificent 17th-18thC square which retains the original façades designed by Hardouin-Mansart. The buildings now house luxury shops and hotels, including the Ritz. At the centre of the square is the Vendôme Column which was built in 1806-10 in the style of Trajan's Column in Rome. It has bronze bas-reliefs celebrating the military exploits of Napoleon (see **A-Z**), with a statue of the emperor himself on top. See **WALK 4**.

**Versailles:** Originally a hunting lodge favoured by Louis XIII, it was transformed into the sumptuous palace we know today by Louis XIV. No expense was spared and building continued for over half a century supervised by the masters Le Vau as architect, Le Brun as decorator and Le Nôtre as garden designer. The latter's task was no easy one as it involved draining the marshy land, diverting the river Bièvre to supply the 1400 fountains and planting 150,000 seedlings. After the Revolution the castle fell into disrepair, the furniture was sold and the paintings removed. It was saved by King Louis-Philippe, who created the Museum of the History of France there in 1837, and restoration work has continued ever since, particularly from the 1950s. See **EXCURSION 3.**

**Accidents & Breakdowns:** If an accident occurs and no-one has been injured, you should fill in the *constat à l'amiable* form with full details. Make sure it is signed by both parties and sent to the appropriate insurance companies. You might check with your own insurance company to see if they have similar forms for use in France. If somebody has been injured, contact the police immediately (see **Emergency Numbers**).
*Breakdowns:* AA and RAC members are entitled to use the services of the Automobile Club de France (6 pl. de la Concorde, 8e) and the Touring Club de France (65 av. de la Grande Armée, 16e). The RAC has a Paris office at 8 pl. Vendôme, 1er. You can obtain a list of emergency breakdown points from motoring clubs in Britain. See **Consulates**, **Driving**.

**Accommodation:** Although there are hundreds of hotels in Paris, it is always advisable to book in advance, especially during peak periods, which include Easter, June, Sep. and Oct. The French Government Tourist Offices (see **Tourist Information**) issue a list of the most heavily booked periods, based on dates of trade fairs, etc.
Hotels – there are five categories: * (basic), ** (comfortable), *** (very comfortable), **** (high class) and ***** (luxury). A double room costs anything between 150F-1000F a night. The more expensive hotels are situated in the 1er, 2e, 8e, 16e and 17e arrondissements (see **A-Z**); the cheaper, more basic hotels are on the Left Bank (see **A-Z**). A complete list of hotels, *Annuaire des Hôtels et Pensions*, is available from French Tourist Offices.
You will find booking facilities at the main Tourist Office, 127 av. des Champs Elysées, 8e, and at Gare d'Austerlitz, Gare du Nord, Gare de l'Est and Gare de Lyon. They offer help with last-minute difficulties but don't necessarily guarantee the best deal. For young people, Accueil des Jeunes en France will assist in finding low-cost accommodation; you'll find branches at 119 rue St. Martin, 4e, and 139 bd. St. Michel, 5e. Both are open 0930-1900 Mon.-Sat. Other branches are at Gare du Nord and 16 rue du Pont Louis-Philippe, 4e, but these are closed Nov.-Feb.
For bed and breakfast accommodation, contact Paris Rêveries at

179 bd. Voltaire, 11e. A double room in a B&B will cost about 180F. Student halls of residence are available July-Sep. and can be booked through Accueil des Jeunes en France. See **Camping & Caravanning**, **Youth Hostels**.

**Airports:** Paris has two international airports: Charles de Gaulle (CDG), at Roissy, 27 km northeast of the city; and Orly South and West, 14 km to the south. CDG has two terminals, with a free shuttle bus between. Both airports have all the usual facilities, which include banks, currency exchange, medical services, car rental, SNCF desk (see **Railways**), restaurants and bars.
From Charles de Gaulle: Air France coaches run to Porte Maillot every 15 min between 0545 and 2300 (journey takes 45 min). For Roissy-Rail, take the shuttle to the railway station and then the RER (see **Railways**) to Gare du Nord (every 15 min, 0500-2315, journey takes 35 min). For RATP buses, service 350 runs from the airport terminals to Gare de l'Est and Gare du Nord, and service 351 goes to pl. de la Nation (journey takes 45-60 min).
From Orly: Air France coaches run to Gare des Invalides or take the Orly bus to M/RER Denfert Rochereau; both leave every 15 min, 0600-2300 (journey takes 35 min). Alternatively take the Orly Rail, RER line C, trains to Gare d'Austerlitz, every 15 min from 0530 to 2330.

**Baby-sitters:** *gardes d'enfants*. ABABA, La Maman en Plus!, tel: 45494646, 0800-2200 (English speakers available); Allo Maman Poule, tel: 47480101, 0900-2000 Mon.-Sat. Prices are 26F per hr plus an agency fee and fares for taxis after 2400. See **Children**.

**Banks:** See **Currency**, **Money**, **Opening Times**.

**Bicycle & Motorcycle Hire:** The traffic in Paris can be extremely dangerous, making the use of either unadvisable. If you do decide to hire, however, you will have to produce a passport or identity card, and proof of a Paris address. A crash helmet is compulsory for mopeds, and as helmets are not provided you must find one yourself. The minimum age for hiring a moped is 18. A refundable deposit is required. For bicycle hire, contact Paris-Vélo, which is located at 2 rue du Fer-à-Moulin, 5e, tel: 43375922. 1000-1300, 1400-1900 Mon.-Sat.; 80F-140F per day.

**Budget:**

| | |
|---|---|
| Inexpensive | One night in a youth hostel: 53F |
| | Meal in a fixed-price menu restaurant: 70F |
| | Meal in a fast-food restaurant: 35F |
| | Transport (*carte orange*): 43F per week |
| Moderate | One night in a two-star hotel: 300F |
| | Two average fixed-price menu meals: 200F |
| | Transport (*billet de tourisme*): 150F per week |
| Expensive | One night in a four-star hotel: 1000F |
| | Two meals in a good restaurant: 600F |
| | Cabaret (without dinner): 350F |

**Buses:** The city bus service is run by RATP, as is the Métro (see **A-Z**), and it is both efficient and easy to use. Bus stops are painted red and yellow, with route numbers clearly marked, and the bus shelters have maps showing the routes, times and fares – each bus has its route number displayed on the front, back and side. All buses operate from 0700-2030, and some run until 2400. You can obtain route maps free from any Métro station. A night bus service runs hourly from pl. du Châtelet. Reduced services operate on Sun. Bus tickets are the same as on the Métro. Punch your ticket (*compostez votre billet*) in the machine beside the driver, or if you have a *carte orange* or *billet de tourisme*, just show it to him. The cost is one or two tickets depending on the length of your journey. RATP also runs excursions to locations outside the city. For a brochure, contact RATP offices or railway stations. See **Transport**.

**Cameras & Photography:** You will find good-quality film and equipment readily available. A fast processing service is offered by the FNAC shop, *niveau* (level) 3, Forum des Halles, 1er. Check with staff before using a camera in museums or art galleries, as there are usually restrictions. In the Musée du Louvre (see **A-Z**), for example, hand-held cameras are admitted free but you will have to pay if you wish to use a tripod, and flashes are prohibited.

**Camping & Caravanning:** There is only one site in the city itself: Camping Île de France, allée du Bord-de-l'Eau, tel: 42241675, 16e, in the Bois de Boulogne. M Porte Maillot. It has 500 places but is usually full in summer. For information on sites around Paris, contact Camping Club de France, 218 bd. St. Germain, 7e, or Fédération Française de Camping et Caravaning, 78 rue de Rivoli, 4e.

**Car Hire:** To hire a car you must produce a passport and a current driving licence which has been valid for at least one year. A cash deposit is necessary, unless paying by credit card, and also proof of a Paris address. The minimum age is 21-25, depending on the company. Be sure to check the basis of charge, i.e. a daily rate plus so much per kilometre, or unlimited mileage. Third-party insurance is compulsory and generally included in the price. For full details contact the Tourist Office (see **Tourist Information**).

| | |
|---|---|
| Avis | 5 rue Bixio, 7e, tel: 45503231. |
| Europcar | 145 av. Malakoff, 16e, tel: 45000806 (many offices). |

**Chemists:** There are plenty of chemists (easily identified by their green cross signs) throughout the city. Most open 1400-1930 Mon., 0900-1930 Tue.-Sat. For addresses of those which open late and on Sun., see the notice displayed on each chemist's door.
A chemist which is open 24 hr is Pharmacie Les Champs, 84 av. des Champs Elysées, 8e. M Franklin D. Roosevelt. For English-speaking staff contact Pharmacie Anglaise, 62 av. des Champs Elysées, 8e (closed Sun.). M Franklin D. Roosevelt.

**Children:** Children are usually made welcome by Parisians. You can quite happily take them to hotels, restaurants, cafés and museums, and there are plenty of activities for them. For information consult *Pariscope* (see **Newspapers**, **What's On**) or contact Loisirs-Jeunes, 36 rue de Ponthieu, 8e, or Paris Junior, 26 rue Delambre, 14e. See **CHILDREN**, **Baby-sitters**.

**Climate:** The nature of the seasons in Paris is similar to that in other northern European cities: winters are relatively mild (mean temp. Nov.-Feb. is 5°C) and dry but cold spells can send the temperature below zero. Springtime is fairly cool and dry. In summer the mean temperature is 18°C but rainfall is greatest during the summer and autumn months so come prepared.

**Complaints:** If you have been overcharged or find that prices do not correspond to those displayed, ask to see the owner or manager of the premises. If you are still not satisfied, you can report the establishment to a Tourist Office (see **Tourist Information**) or the police (see **A-Z**) but you will find that threatening this course of action is usually sufficient.

**Consulates:**
UK Embassy – 35 rue du Faubourg St. Honoré, 8e, tel: 42669142
Consulate – 16 rue d'Anjou, 8e, tel: 42669142
Australia – 4 rue Jean-Rey, 15e, tel: 40593305
Canada – 35 av. Montaigne, 8e, tel: 47230101
New Zealand – 7 rue Léonard-de-Vinci, 16e, tel: 45002411
USA – 2 av. Gabriel, 8e, tel: 42961202

**Conversion Chart:**

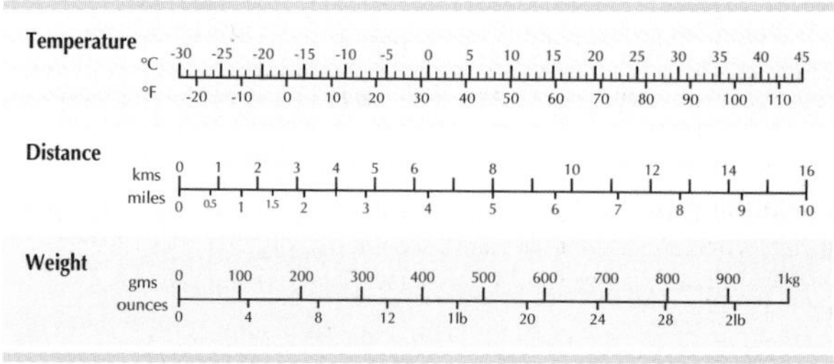


**Credit Cards:** See **Money**.

**Crime & Theft:** Special care should always be taken of handbags and wallets, etc., as pickpockets are rife on the Métro, buses and in all crowded locations. Never leave your car unlocked and be sure to remove or hide any valuables. If you do have anything stolen, report the theft immediately to the nearest police station (*commissariat de police*) and obtain an *attestation de vol* document so you can claim insurance (see **A-Z**). You must inform your embassy at once if your passport is stolen (see **Consulates**). See **Emergency Numbers**, **Police**.

**Currency:** The French unit of currency is the franc which is divided into 100 centimes. Banknotes are issued for 500F, 200F, 100F, 50F and 20F. Coins are 10F (two types, the older version is bronze-coloured, the newer ones are smaller with a brass rim and silver centre), 5F, 2F, 1F, 50c (all silver), 20c, 10c and 5c (all brass). See **Money**.

**Customs Allowances:**

| Duty Paid Into: | Cigarettes (or) | Cigars (or) | Tobacco | Spirits | Wine |
|---|---|---|---|---|---|
| EC | 300 | 75 | 400 g | 1.5 *l* | 5 *l* |
| UK | 300 | 75 | 400 g | 1.5 *l* | 5 *l* |

**Disabled People:** For information about accommodation, transport, facilities and aids for the disabled, see the booklet *Touristes Quand Même* supplied by the Tourist Office (see **Tourist Information**). See **Health**, **Insurance**.

**Drinks:** In France there are no licensing laws, so you can buy alcohol in bars and cafés at any time. House wines are sold by the litre (*une*

*carafe*), half-litre (*un demi-litre*) or quarter litre (*un quart*); a jug (*un pichet*) can hold either a quarter or half-litre. Beer is usually lager, although you will find a wider selection if you go to a 'pub'. It is quite alright to ask for plain water (*une carafe d'eau*) with a meal, and this comes free. If you want a small, strong, black espresso coffee ask for *un café*; *un café au lait* for coffee with milk; and *un grand crème* for a large white coffee, the kind usually served at breakfast with croissants. Tea is growing in popularity, with the best being available at the special *salons de thé*. Otherwise it tends to be pretty awful! Hot chocolate is simply *un chocolat.*
In cafés it is less expensive to stand at the bar (*au comptoir*) than to sit down with your coffee and croissants, etc. There is also sometimes a difference in price between inside and outside the café, i.e. at a table on the pavement.

**Driving:** Driving in Paris can be a hair-raising experience and is not recommended. If you intend to travel to Paris by car, you will need a valid national or international driving licence plus insurance documents (a Green Card is no longer necessary for EC members but the AA recommends that you have one anyway), nationality sticker, yellow filters for headlamps and a red warning triangle. You should, whenever possible, use the ring road (*boulevard périphérique*) rather than attempt to drive across the city.
The French drive on the right-hand side of the road, and at T-junctions, intersections and roundabouts the traffic from the right has right-of-way. Cars should be equipped with seat belts and these should be worn at all times in both the front and the back seats. The only exception applies to children under 10 in cars that are not fitted with a special child's seat (these will be compulsory from Jan. 1993).
*Speed-limits:* built-up areas 50 kph; Paris ring road 80 kph; main roads 90/110 kph; motorways (*autoroutes*) 130 kph.
See **Accidents & Breakdowns**, **Car Hire**, **Parking**, **Petrol**.

**Drugs:** In France it is illegal to use or possess any form of narcotics, and anyone caught trying to smuggle drugs into the country faces almost certain imprisonment.

**Eating Out:** This is one of the most enjoyable facets of Parisian life, and need not cost you a fortune either. By law, all restaurants must display their prices outside and have at least one fixed-price menu (*menu fixe* or *formule*) as well as the à la carte. These fixed-price menus can cost as little as 50F, whereas the à la carte is always slightly more expensive. Paris caters for all tastes and budgets, ranging from international and *nouvelle cuisine* to traditional French provincial cooking. Contact the Tourist Office (see **Tourist Information**) for the useful free booklet, *Guide des Restaurants de Paris.*

Restaurants traditionally open 1200-1400, 1900-2200; alternatively you can grab a quick meal in a brasserie at almost any time. Bistros are similar to brasseries but are usually cheaper, with a set meal of the day, basic food and quick service.

Cafés serve a variety of drinks all day, as well as snacks such as croissants and *croque-monsieur* (a type of cheese and ham toasted sandwich). *Salons de thé* specialize in rather expensive pots of tea with cakes and rich pastries. Remember that it will cost less to stand at the bar or to eat inside than to sit at a table outside.

If you require a late-night snack try a *drugstore*, which provides a similar service to that of a brasserie, but is open till 0200. See RESTAURANTS 1-4, **Food**.

**Electricity:** The voltage in Paris is 220 V, which is fine for most UK appliances, but plugs and sockets vary greatly and are completely different from those in Britain, so an adaptor is essential (available from most electrical shops).

**Emergency Numbers:**

| | |
|---|---|
| Police | 17 |
| Fire Brigade | 18 |
| SAMU (24 hr ambulance) | 45675050 |
| SOS Médecins (24 hr emergency doctor) | 43377777 |
| SOS Dentistes (24 hr emergency dentist) | 43375100 |
| Emergency treatment for poisoning | 40370404 |
| Emergency treatment for serious burns | 42341212 |
| Rape Crisis Hotline (English speakers ask for Anne) | 05059595 |
| SOS HELP English Crisis Hotline (1500-2300) | 47238080 |

**Events:** The Tourist Office (see **Tourist Information**) issues a list of all city events and a monthly leaflet on the major ones (*Paris Sélection*).
*January*: Winter sales in the shops; International Boat Show at CNIT, La Défense (2nd or 3rd week).
*March:* Agricultural Show, Parc des Expositions, Porte de Versailles.
*April:* Opening of Foire de Paris (Paris Fair) at Parc des Expositions, Porte de Versailles (late April/early May).
*May:* Labour Day (1st); celebration of Allied Victory 1945 (8th); Paris Air Show at Le Bourget (late May/early June); Soirées de St. Aignan, at Hôtel St Aignan, 18th-19thC European music.
*June:* Flower Show in the floral gardens, Bois de Vincennes (see **A-Z**); Festival du Marais, theatre, dance, mime, music (Marais district, mid-June/mid-July); Summer Solstice (21st) parades (inc. Gay Pride March), street entertainment, etc.; Festival International de Film Fantastique et de Science-Fiction, at Grand Rex cinema, 1 bd. Poissonière, 2e.
*July:* Bastille Day (see **Quatorze Juillet**); Paris Summer Music Festival

(mid-July/mid-Sep.).
*September:* Festival d'Automne, music, drama (Sep.-Dec.).
*October:* Festival Internationale de Danse de Paris, at Théâtre des Champs Elysées (see MUSIC VENUES); Festival d'Art Sacré, religious music, church concerts (Oct.-Nov.); Montmartre Wine Festival, rue des Saules/rue St. Vincent (1st or 2nd week); International Contemporary Art Exhibition (FIAC), Grand Palais (early Oct.-Dec.); Festival de Jazz (late Oct.-early Nov.).
*November:* All Saints' Day (1st); Armistice Day (11th), Arc de Triomphe.
*December:* Midnight Mass in principal churches (24th).

**Health:** Medical treatment through the French social security system is available to all citizens of EC countries. Residents of the UK should obtain a form E 111 from the DSS before leaving. Be warned, you will have to pay for any treatment in the first instance then claim it back afterwards, which can be a time-consuming, complicated affair. Even an ordinary visit to the doctor costs about 85F so it certainly pays to take out medical insurance beforehand. Lists of doctors (including those available on Sun. and hols) can be obtained from hotels, chemists or police stations.
American Hospital – 63 bd. Victor Hugo, Neuilly-sur-Seine, tel: 47475300 (English-speaking)
British Hospital – 3 rue Barbès, Levallois-Perret, tel: 47581312
See **Disabled People**, **Emergency Numbers**, **Insurance**.

**Insurance:** You should take out travel insurance covering you against theft and loss of property and money, as well as medical expenses, for the duration of your stay. Your travel agent should be able to recommend a suitable policy. See **Crime & Theft**, **Driving**, **Health**.

**Laundries:** Hotels are generally happy to do your laundry; otherwise you will find many self-service coin-operated Launderettes around the city (*blanchisserie-self*). Launderettes in the city centre can be found at 28 rue Beaubourg, 3e, 96 rue St. Antoine, 4e, and 3 rue de la Montagne Ste Geneviève, 5e.

METROPOLITAIN
AZ DE
The California

**Lost Property:** Contact the Bureau des Objets Trouvés, 36 rue des Morillons, 15e, tel: 45311480. 0830-1700 Mon.-Fri. (till 2000 Tue. & Thu.). M Convention. The airports (see **A-Z**) and major railway stations (see **Railways**) also have their own lost-property offices.

**Métro:** Parisians have used the Métro since the start of the century (19 July 1900 to be precise) and its 15 lines and 360 stations save much time and are extremely convenient. It is open 0530-0030 and dotted all over the city you'll see the distinctive Art Nouveau entrance signs. Maps may be obtained free from all stations and Tourist Offices (see **Tourist Information**).
Tickets and special passes are available from RATP booths at the entrance to stations and from the SNCF desk at Charles de Gaulle airport (see **A-Z**). A tourist ticket (*billet de tourisme/Paris sésame*) will give you seven days' unlimited travel on the Métro, RER and bus (but not RER Roissy Rail), first class only; 150F. The *carte orange* (orange card) is very popular with Parisians and combines an ID card with a passport photo. This lets you buy a weekly ticket for unlimited travel on the Métro or bus (valid Mon. am to Sun. eve) for 43F or monthly for about 180F. A *formule 1* ticket will provide you with unlimited travel up to Zone 3 on the Métro and bus for one day and costs 19F.
For short stays a *carnet* of ten tickets (32,80F) often works out cheaper, with a flat rate of one ticket per journey (remember to retain it till the end of your journey – an inspector may ask to see it).

**Money:** The two main banks are BNP (Banque National de Paris) and CL (Crédit Lyonnais). 0900-1700 Mon.-Fri. Banks which open on Sat. include Crédit Commercial de France, 115 av. des Champs Elysées, 8e (0900-2000) and BNP, 1 bd. Haussmann, 9e (0900-1200).
There are exchange facilities at airports and mainline railway stations, plus many *bureaux de change* in the centre of the city. Some banks, but not all, will also change money and traveller's cheques. Exchange rates and commission charges vary from bank to bank so it pays to look around. For a late-opening exchange try Société Financière de Change Lincoln, 11 rue Lincoln, 8e. 1000-2000.
Credit cards are widely accepted, with Visa (*Carte Bleu*) being the most

common, so look out for the appropriate signs on doors and windows. The American Express office is at 11 rue Scribe, 9e, tel: 47777707. 0900-1730 Mon.-Sat. M Opéra.
Traveller's cheques are probably the safest way to carry holiday money, and can be used in a great many locations, though not in some of the cheaper hotels and restaurants. You will find them easy to exchange at any bank or *bureau de change*. See **Crime & Theft**, **Currency**.

**Museums:** A Carte Musée et Monuments (Museums and Monuments Pass) is available for 65 Parisian museums and can be obtained in 1-day, 3-day and 5-day versions. The cost ranges from 55F to 160F and it can be obtained from Métro stations, TouristOffices (see **A-Z**) and the museums and monuments involved in the scheme. The pass can also be bought in advance in the UK by contacting Voyages Vacances International Ltd, 4th Floor, 197 Knightsbridge, London SW7 1RB, tel: 071-5896769. See **ART GALLERIES, MUSEUMS 1-3**.

**Newspapers:** You can buy newspapers at pavement news-kiosks, bookshops and drugstores. The French dailies include: *Le Monde,* which is authoritative, slightly left-of-centre and has no pictures; *Le Figaro*, conservative; and *Libération*, independent and left-wing. British papers and the *International Herald Tribune* are all widely available at kiosks in the centre of Paris. It is also possible to purchase British magazines at W. H. Smith in av. des Champs Elysées. See **What's On**.

**Nightlife:** There is plenty of nightlife in Paris, ranging from the world-famous cabarets, like the Lido, Moulin Rouge (see **A-Z**) or Folies Bergère, to nightclubs, discos, jazz clubs and bars. The most lively areas include St. Germain-des-Prés, Les Halles, the Latin Quarter (see **A-Z**), rue Mouffetard (see **A-Z**), Montparnasse (see **A-Z**), Montmartre (see **A-Z**), Pigalle (see **A-Z**) and the Champs Elysées (see **A-Z**). See **NIGHTLIFE**.

**Opening Times:**
Banks – 0900-1200, 1400-1630 Mon.-Fri. (busy central branches stay

open at lunchtime).
Post offices – 0800-1900 Mon.-Fri., 0800-1200 Sat.
Offices – 0830-1200, 1400-1800 Mon.-Sat.
Restaurants – Generally open 1200-1500, 1930-2230. Many close Mon. and some close for the whole of Aug.
Shops – 1000-1900 Tue.-Sat. (department stores open Mon.).

**Orientation:** The city is divided from east to west by the river Seine, with the Right Bank to the north and Left Bank to the south. At the city centre are the islands of Île de la Cité and Île St. Louis, and the cathedral of Notre-Dame de Paris. The main axis of the city lies on the Right Bank from the Musée du Louvre through the Arc de Triomphe to La Défense. Montmartre with Sacré-Coeur is to the north of the centre; Tour Maine-Montparnasse is to the south and the Tour Eiffel to the west. If you use these three landmarks as a guide you should always be able to find out roughly where you are in the city.

**Parking:** Parking in the city tends to be very restricted, so try the underground car parks in the city centre and at all the major *portes* on the ring road (and then take the Métro into the centre). Parking meters operate 0900-1900, and traffic wardens and police can impose hefty fines or tow away illegally parked vehicles. If your car is impounded, you will have to telephone the town hall (*mairie*) in that arrondissement (see **A-Z**) to reclaim it. See **Driving**.

**Passports & Customs:** A passport from Britain, Ireland or the EC allows a 90-day stay and no visa is required. Also acceptable are British Visitor's Passports and Excursion Passes (available from post offices). If you wish to stay for more than 90 days, contact the local police station in France, or Préfecture de Police (Service des Etrangers), 163 rue de Charenton, Paris, 12e, tel: 43418149. Citizens from other countries, including Australia and New Zealand, require a visa, which is easily obtained from French embassies and consulates in those countries. Australia: Consulate, St. Martin Tower, 31 Manet St, Sydney NSW 2000, tel: 3281250. Embassy in Canberra, consulate in Melbourne. Canada: Embassy, 42 Promenade Sussex, Ottawa, Ontario K1M 2C9,

tel: 5121715. Consulates in Toronto, Edmonton and Montreal.
New Zealand: Embassy, 1 Williston St, DBP 1695, Wellington, tel: 720200.
UK: Embassy, 58 Knightsbridge, London SW1, tel: 2358080. Consulates in Liverpool and Edinburgh.
USA: Embassy, 4101 Reservoir Rd NY, Washington DC, 20007, tel: 9446000. Consulates in Boston, Chicago, Miami, New York and San Francisco.

**Petrol:** *l'essence*. There are plenty of petrol stations around the city, though most are not self-service. See **Driving**.

**Police:** The police can be recognized by their dark blue uniforms and flat caps. Always address them as 'Monsieur l'Agent' – they are usually considerate to tourists. Any theft should be reported to the nearest police station (*commissariat de police*). The Police Headquarters in Paris is at 51 pl. du Marché St. Honoré, 1er. See **Crime & Theft, Emergency Numbers**.

**Post Offices:** They can be identified by their yellow signs marked 'PTT' or 'Postes', and provide full postal facilities as well as telephones for both local and long-distance calls. These can be metered and paid for afterwards (see **Telephones & Telegrams**). Postage stamps can also be purchased from *tabacs*. Parisian letter boxes are painted yellow. Any mail to be picked up should be clearly addressed with your name and 'Poste Restante', then sent to Paris Louvre (see below). You will have to produce your passport before collecting any mail.
The Head Post Office (open 24 hr) is at Paris Louvre, 52 rue du Louvre, 1er. M Louvre, M/RER Châtelet-Les Halles.

**Public Holidays:** 1 Jan.; Easter Sun. and Mon.; Ascension (40 days after Easter); Pentecost (7th Sun. after Easter plus following Mon.); 1 May (Labour Day); 8 May (Armistice Day 1945); 14 July (Bastille Day – see **Quatorze Juillet**); 15 Aug. (Assumption of Virgin Mary); 1 Nov. (All Saints' Day); 11 Nov. (Armistice Day 1918); 25 Dec. (Christmas Day).

**Rabies:** Still exists here as in other parts of the Continent. As a precaution have all animal bites seen to immediately by a doctor.

**Railways:** The RER (Réseau Express Régional/Regional Express Network) is linked to the Métro (see **A-Z**) and has three lines (A, B and C) connecting the city to the suburbs and outlying areas. Note that for Zone 1 it uses the same ticket system as the Métro (supplementary tickets are required for travel to the suburbs).
The SNCF (Société Nationale des Chemins de Fer Français) is the national network, which provides a fast, comfortable service. Paris has six main-line stations: Gare du Nord (for Boulogne, Calais, Belgium, Holland, Scandinavia); Gare de l'Est (for eastern France, Germany, Switzerland, Austria); Gare St. Lazare (for Dieppe, Normandy); Gare de Lyon (for the Alps, south of France, Italy, Greece); Gare d'Austerlitz (for the southwest, Spain, Portugal); Gare Montparnasse (for Brittany, Versailles, Chartres, Atlantic coast).
Stations have all the usual facilities, including currency exchange, shops and Tourist Offices. Reservations are recommended for long-distance journeys and you can buy either first- or second-class tickets. You must then punch the ticket in the machine on the platform before boarding the train. If you don't do this and are asked to produce the ticket by an inspector, you may be charged for another one. For general railway enquiries, tel: 42615050.

**Religious Services:** France is predominantly a Catholic country and details and times of services can be obtained from the Centre d'Information et de Documentation Religieuse, 8 rue Massillon, 4e, tel: 46330101.
Anglican: St. George's Church, 7 rue Auguste Vacquerie, 16e.
Church of Scotland: 17 rue Bayard, 8e.
Protestant: American Church, 65 quai d'Orsay, 7e.
Jewish: Association Israélite de Paris, 17 rue St. Georges, 9e.
Muslim: Mosquée de Paris, pl. du Puits-de-l'Ermite, 5e.

**Shopping:** Paris has something for everyone – even those who don't enjoy shopping – from the bookstalls (*bouquinistes*) along the Seine

(see **A-Z**) to the exclusive fashion houses (see **Fashion**). The main shopping areas are Les Halles (all kinds), bd. Haussmann (department stores), rue Faubourg St. Honoré (high fashion), rue Royale (expensive jewellery), rue de Rivoli (perfume and souvenirs) and, on the Left Bank (see **A-Z**), St. Germain-des-Prés (books, antiques, art and fashion). See **MARKETS, SHOPPING 1-3.**

**Smoking:** Smoking is tolerated less and less in public places in Paris. It is not permitted on public transport or in food shops, department stores, cinemas, theatres, museums and art galleries. Some restaurants now have no-smoking areas. In general it is better to avoid smoking in public places altogether.

**Sports:** Details of current sports events and facilities are well covered in *Pariscope* or *Paris Passion* (see **What's On**), or the telephone information service Allô Sports, tel: 42765454.
Rugby internationals in Feb. and Mar. at Parc des Princes, 24 rue du Commandant Guilbaud, 16e.

International Tennis Championships in June at Stade Roland-Garros, av. Gordon Bennett, 16e.
Finish of the Tour de France cycle race in mid-July along the av. des Champs Elysées.
Horse racing at Longchamp (Prix de l'Arc de Triomphe and Prix de la République in Oct.) and Auteuil (see **Bois de Boulogne**); trotting races at Vincennes (Aug.-Sep.).

**Taxis:** Paris boasts 14,300 official taxis which can be either picked up at one of the numerous taxi ranks or ordered by telephone. Within the *boulevard périphérique* (ring road) there are two tariffs: A – 2,55F per km, 0700-2000; B – 3,97F per km, 2000-0700 and all day Sun. and hols. For trips outside the ring road, tariff B applies 0700-2000 and tariff C (5,33F per km) 2000-0700. Supplementary charges of 3F or 4F apply for taxis at main-line railway stations, for luggage and for more than three passengers. It should be noted that tipping (see **A-Z**) is normal but not obligatory.
G7 Radio, tel: 47394739
Taxis-Bleus, tel: 49361010
Alpha-Taxis, tel: 45858585

**Telephones & Telegrams:** You will find numerous payphones but you may have difficulty finding one that accepts money rather than phonecards. Coin-operated telephones take 1F, 5F and occasionally 10F coins. Phonecards (*télécartes*) are available from post offices and *tabacs* and cost 45F and 96F. To use a cardphone, lift the receiver, insert the card, pull down the handle above it and dial. For coin-operated telephones, insert the money first then dial. In post offices (see **A-Z**) you can use a metered telephone which lets you make the call before paying. If using a café telephone you may have to buy a *jeton* (token) at the bar.
When dialling inside Paris you need only use the eight digits. For calls to the rest of the country dial 16 and then the area code and number. For international calls dial 19, wait for the dialling tone, then dial the country code (44 for UK, 61 for Australia, 11 for USA), followed by the area code (omitting the initial zero) and number. If you wish to make a

reverse-charge call abroad, dial 1933 then the country code to get through to a bilingual operator. You can receive return calls at telephone booths.
A telegram service is available at post offices. By telephone inside France, tel: 3655 and dictate (in French). For abroad, tel: 42332111 (in English).

**Television & Radio:** There are six channels on French TV: TF1, A2, FR3, LA5, M6 and Canal+ (the first paying and coded network). By 1992 cable TV will be catering for as many as 30 channels. The news is broadcast at 0800, 1300, 2000 and 2300.
French radio broadcasts in French on FM. The best-known stations are: France-Inter, France Musique, France Culture, Radio Tour Eiffel, Skyrock, NRJ, Radio Classique, RTL and Europe 1. It is possible to receive BBC Radio 4 by tuning in to 1500 m long wave and BBC World Service on 463 m medium wave. All Parisian FM radio stations are listed in *Pariscope* (see **What's On**).

**Time Difference:** French standard time is GMT plus 1 hr and the clocks go forward 1 hr in summer, making France (like the rest of Western Europe) always 1 hr ahead of Britain.

**Tipping:** A 15% service charge is included in your bill at all hotels and restaurants, so there is no need to leave anything unless you feel the service has been particularly good, in which case a small tip of 10F for the waiter is appropriate. If you pay by cash, any small change is usually left for the waiter. Hotel porters average 10F for each item of luggage, chambermaids 10F per day, taxi drivers 10-15% of the fare, hairdressers about 10F and cinema usherettes 2F.

**Toilets:** Public toilets are few and far between in Paris. Some of the bigger Métro (see **A-Z**) stations have them (e.g. Bastille, Concorde) and also the big shopping centres (e.g. Forum des Halles). Otherwise there are a certain number of automatic lavatories in the street which cost 2F – when they work! Children under 10 should not be allowed to use these alone for safety reasons.

OHEME
AU CLAIRON DES
Carlsberg

**Tourist Information:** The main Tourist Office is at 127 av. des Champs Elysées, 8e, near the Arc de Triomphe. 0900-2200 Mon.-Sat., 0900-1800 Sun. You'll find the staff speak English and are both helpful and friendly. It is well stocked with free maps and leaflets giving information on accommodation, restaurants, exhibitions, entertainments, transport and excursions. You can also buy guidebooks and maps in the bookshop. Other Tourist Offices can be found at the following railway stations: Gare d'Austerlitz, Gare de l'Est, Gare de Lyon and Gare du Nord. Tourist information in English is available by dialling 47208898. The French Government Tourist Office in the UK is at 178 Piccadilly, London W1V 0AL, tel: 071-4996911.

**Transport:** Paris has one of the best public transport systems in the world. The RATP (*Régie Autonome des Transports Parisiens*) runs the interlinked Métro, bus and RER, which serve the city and the suburbs. The system is fast, easy to use and very well signposted – in fact it is almost impossible to get lost on the Métro. Inter-city and international rail services are provided by SNCF from six main-line stations. The two airports which serve Paris are connected to the city by a fast and frequent bus and rail service. See **Airports**, **Buses**, **Métro**, **Railways**, **Taxis**.

**Traveller's Cheques:** See **Money**.

**What's On:** The most useful listings publications are *Pariscope* (weekly, 3F, in French) and *l'Officiel des Spectacles* (weekly, 2F, in French). They are both available every Wed. You'll also find the magazine *Paris Passion* helpful (bi-monthly, in English). All are easily obtained from kiosks and newsagents. See **Newspapers**.

**Youth Hostels:** The YHA in France is the Fédération Unie des Auberges de Jeunesse, 27 rue Pajol, 75018 Paris, tel: 46070001. There are two hostels in the city itself, though you have to hold an international YHA membership to use them. The cost is 82F per night, which includes breakfast. They are:
Jules Ferry, 8 bd. Jules Ferry, 11e, tel: 43575560. M République.
D'Artagnon, 80 rue Vitruve, 20e, tel: 43610875. M Porte de Bagnolet.
The youth organization Accueil des Jeunes en France (AJF) also runs a chain of fine city hostels costing 90F per night. Although no membership is necessary for these, they are restricted to 18-30s and don't accept bookings ahead, so be prepared to take a chance.
AJF hostels:
Résidence Bastille, 151 av. Ledru-Rollin, 11e, tel: 43795386.
M Bastille, Voltaire.
Le Fourcy, 6 rue de Fourcy, 4e, tel: 42742345. M St. Paul.
Le Fauconnier, 11 rue du Fauconnier, 4e, tel: 42742345. M Pont Marie.
Maubuisson, 12 rue des Barres, 4e, tel: 42727209. M Hôtel de Ville.
François Miron, 6 rue François Miron, 4e, tel: 42727209. M Hôtel de Ville.

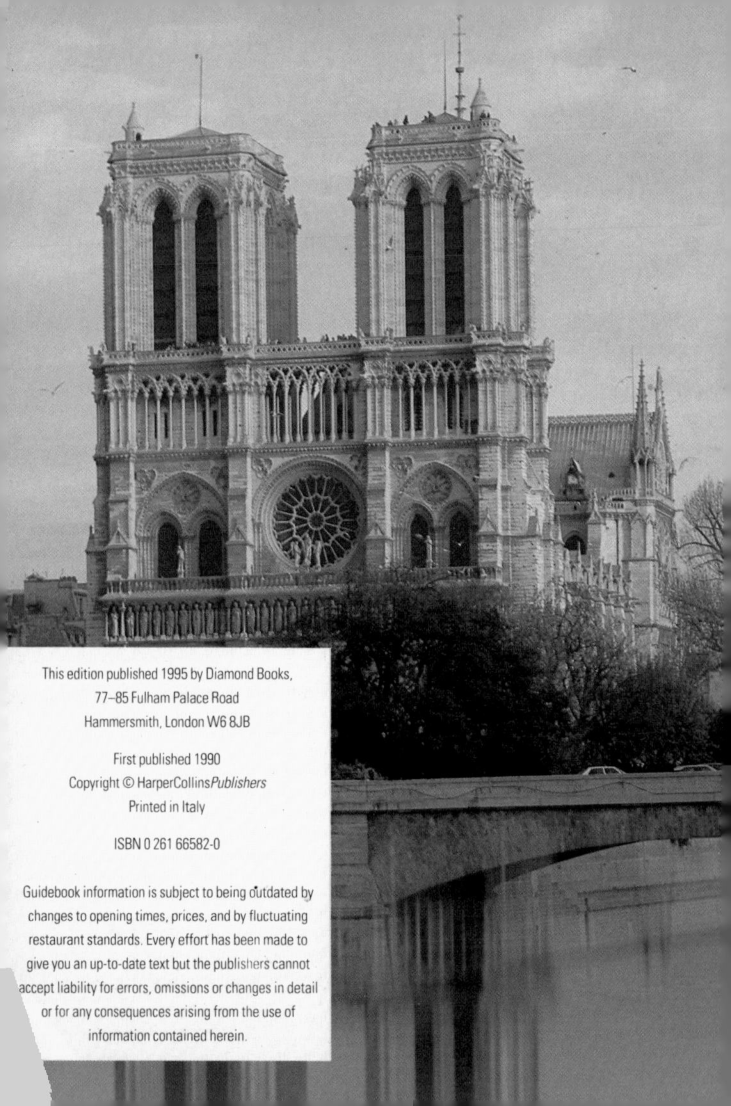

This edition published 1995 by Diamond Books,
77–85 Fulham Palace Road
Hammersmith, London W6 8JB

First published 1990

Printed in Italy

ISBN 0 261 66582-0